HOTSPOTS
GIBRALTAR

Written by Katherine Rushton

Published by Thomas Cook Publishing
A division of Thomas Cook Tour Operations Limited.
Company registration no. 1450464 England
The Thomas Cook Business Park, Unit 9, Coningsby Road,
Peterborough PE3 8SB, United Kingdom
Email: books@thomascook.com, Tel: + 44 (0) 1733 416477
www.thomascookpublishing.com

Produced by Cambridge Publishing Management Limited
Burr Elm Court, Main Street, Caldecote CB23 7NU

ISBN: 978-1-84157-935-1

First edition © 2008 Thomas Cook Publishing
Text © Thomas Cook Publishing,
Maps © Thomas Cook Publishing/PCGraphics (UK) Limited

Series Editor: Diane Ashmore
Production/DTP: Steven Collins

Printed and bound in Spain by GraphyCems

Cover photography by © Jon Arnold Images/Alamy

CONTENTS

WHAT'S IN YOUR GUIDEBOOK?

Independent authors Impartial, up-to-date information from our travel experts who meticulously source local knowledge.

Experience Thomas Cook's 165 years in the travel industry and guidebook publishing enriches every word with expertise you can trust.

Travel know-how Contributions by thousands of staff around the globe, each one living and breathing travel.

Editors Travel-publishing professionals, pulling everything together to craft a perfect blend of words, pictures, maps and design.

You, the traveller We deliver a practical, no-nonsense approach to information, geared to how you really use it.

THE AUTHOR

Katherine Rushton lives in London with her Gibraltarian husband. She works as a full-time journalist for a trade magazine, and occasionally contributes to *Time Out*, the *Telegraph* and the *Guardian*. She used to be resident on the Rock, where she worked for the local newspaper the *Gibraltar Chronicle*.

● *Gibraltar is well known for the apes that live on the Rock*

INTRODUCTION
Getting to know Gibraltar and the surrounding area

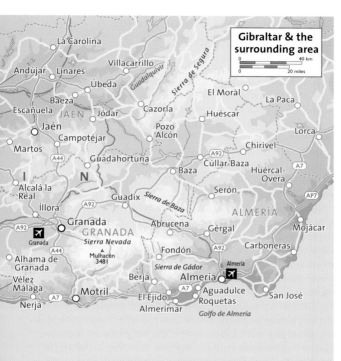

Gibraltar & the surrounding area

| 0 | 40 km |
| 0 | 20 miles |

La Carolina

Andújar   Linares   Villacarrillo

Úbeda   *Guadalquivir*   *Sierra de Segura*

El Moral   La Paca

Baeza   Cazorla   Huéscar

Escañuela   JAÉN   Jódar

Jaén   Pozo   Lorca
   Alcón

Campotéjar   Chirivel

Martos   A44   Guadahortuna   A92   Huércal-
   Baza   Cúllar-Baza   Overa   A7

I   N   AP7

Alcalá la   Sierra de Baza   Serón   ALMERÍA
Real   Guadix
   A92   Abrucena   Gérgal   Mojácar
Íllora

A92   Granada   Carboneras
   GRANADA
Granada   Sierra Nevada   Fondón   A92
   Berja   Almería
A44   Mulhacén   Sierra de Gádor
Alhama de   3481   Almería
Granada   El Ejido   A7   Aguadulce   San José
Vélez   Motril   Almerimar   Roquetas
Málaga   A7   *Golfo de Almería*
Nerja

Mediterranean Sea

○	City
○	Large Town
○	Small Town
■	POI
	Motorway
	Main Road
	Minor Road
✈	Airport
	Railway

France
Portugal   Spain
   Gibraltar
Morocco   Algeria

Getting to know Gibraltar and the surrounding area

Perched at the tip of Europe and dominated by a soaring limestone peak, Gibraltar packs a lot into its very small footprint. At first glance, the Rock – as it is affectionately known – is an old-fashioned British seaside resort given a sunny Mediterranean makeover. Tapas bars jostle for space with pubs and fish and chip restaurants, and narrow streets of whitewashed houses nod to their British standing with painted Union flags. But the Spanish and British cultures are not the only ones competing here. The backstreets are filled with the scent of simmering tagines and shops are crammed with Moroccan dates, spices and flat leather slippers.

Away from the town, the Upper Rock nature reserve is home to Gibraltar's most famous residents, the monkeys, which are tame enough to jump on tourists' shoulders and bold enough to make off with their cameras. The reserve is also the access point for an impressive network of tunnels blasted through the Rock as lookout points and affords unmissable views both to Spain and across the Strait of Gibraltar to Morocco.

Gibraltar is the ideal base for exploring both these places. The Costa del Sol's glamorous holiday playgrounds of Marbella and Puerto Banús are within easy reach, and the historic cities of Ronda and Sevilla are close enough to make satisfying day trips. Stretching to the west of Gibraltar, the Costa de la Luz offers a more bohemian beach holiday in the sleepy fishing villages of Bolonia and Zahara de los Atunes or the kite-surfing Mecca of Tarifa. The winds can be fierce here, but locals are right when they say that a single day of perfect weather on these beaches is worth a whole summer elsewhere.

When the skies are clear here, you can see across the Straits so clearly that you can make out the individual houses in Morocco – which is of course the other great allure of holidaying in Gibraltar. The colourful souks of Tangier are a quick ferry hop away, making a rewarding target for a day trip, or the ideal springboard for exploration further afield.

● *Looking past the tip of the Rock towards the Spanish coast*

THE BEST OF GIBRALTAR & THE SURROUNDING AREA

The Rock is the perfect base from which to explore a diverse range of places.

TOP 10 ATTRACTIONS

- **The Apes' Den** is home of the Rock's famous Barbary macaques – the only wild primates remaining in Europe (see page 16).

- **Great Siege Tunnels** are a vast network of tunnels blasted through by British forces, which helped them triumph in the Great Siege of 1782 (see page 19).

- **Upper Rock Nature Reserve** offers staggering views across the Straits to the Riff Mountains in Morocco, and a paradise for bird lovers (see page 16).

- **Lazing on beaches** is easy, with Gibraltar placed in between the busy resorts of the Costa del Sol and the windswept strands of the Costa de la Luz.

- **Puerto Banús** is Andalucía's most sophisticated marina, with luxury yachts, trendy shops, restaurants and bars (see page 31).

- **Wander around Marbella's Casco Antiguo or Old Town**, with its picturesque main square, the Plaza de los Naranjos (see page 37).

- **Tarifa** Watch kite surfers during the day, then soak up the bohemian atmosphere of Tarifa's Moorish town centre over fresh mint *mojitos* or *caipirinhas* (see page 60).

- **Sevilla**, the atmospheric capital of Andalucía, is home to Europe's largest Gothic cathedral as well as a stunning Moorish Alcazar (see page 74).

- **Ronda** is famous for its bullring, ancient bridge and amazing setting high above the Guadelevin River (see page 80).

- **Lose yourself in the narrow streets of Tangier's medieval souk**, among Berber jewellery, woven rugs and bright earthenware tagines (see page 69).

🔻 *Stunning illuminations in St Michael's Cave*

SYMBOLS KEY

The following symbols are used throughout this book:

ⓐ address ☎ telephone ⓦ website address ⓔ email
🕐 opening times ❶ important

The following symbols are used on the maps:

𝒊	information office	○	city
✉	post office	○	large town
🛍	shopping	○	small town
✈	airport	■	POI (point of interest)
➕	hospital	═	motorway
🛡	police station	—	main road
🚌	bus station	—	minor road
🚆	railway station	—	railway
✝	church		

❶ numbers denote featured cafés, restaurants & evening venues

RESTAURANT CATEGORIES

The symbol after the name of each restaurant listed in this guide indicates the price of a typical three-course meal without drinks for one person:

£ under €12   ££ €12–45   £££ more than €45

▶ *Gibraltar's beaches offer warm, clear waters and plenty of sun*

RESORTS
Places under the sun

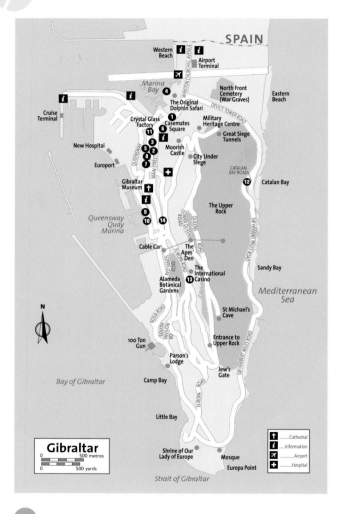

SPAIN

Western Beach

Airport Terminal

Marina Bay

4

The Original Dolphin Safari

North Front Cemetery (War Graves)

Eastern Beach

Cruise Terminal

Crystal Glass Factory

11

6

1 Casemates Square

Military Heritage Centre

Great Siege Tunnels

New Hospital

3
9 **2**
8
7

Moorish Castle

City Under Siege

Europort

Gibraltar Museum

Catalan Bay Road

Catalan Bay

12

Queensway Quay Marina

5
9
10 **14**

The Upper Rock

Cable Car

The Apes' Den

Sandy Bay

Alameda Botanical Gardens

The International Casino

13

Mediterranean Sea

St Michael's Cave

100 Ton Gun

Entrance to Upper Rock

Bay of Gibraltar

Parson's Lodge

Camp Bay

Jew's Gate

Little Bay

Shrine of Our Lady of Europe

Mosque

Europa Point

Strait of Gibraltar

N

Gibraltar

| 0 | | 500 metres |
| 0 | | 500 yards |

✝	.....Cathedral
ℹ	.....Information
✈	.....Airport
✚	.....Hospital

Gibraltar

Gibraltar – or 'Gib' as it is more colloquially known – is dominated by a soaring chunk of limestone that stands over 420 m (1,390 ft) high and guards over the narrow entrance to the Mediterranean. This strategic position is also the key to its chequered past. The Rock was first inhabited by the Phoenicians, who used it a landmark signalling the entrance to the Mediterranean, then by a variety of invaders and finally by the Moors. The Moorish leader Tarik gave it its present name, derived from *Gebel Tarik* which means Tarik's Mountain in Arabic.

Since then, Gibraltar has been repeatedly fought over by the Spanish and the British, who finally conquered the territory more than 300 years ago in 1704. But the issue of sovereignty is still very much a live one, and Gibraltarians show fierce loyalty to their British colonisers. Backstreets are decorated with Union flags; many older Gibraltarians refuse to cross the border into Spain; and every year 10 September is given over to a highly political 'national day' celebration, when the entire population of 30,000 turns out in the colours of the Gibraltar flag, red and white.

Certainly Gibraltar is very like a British town to look at. The street furniture, signposts, phone boxes, food, currency and pubs are all British – but the climate and the beaches are decidedly Mediterranean, making it a popular destination for British expats. It is also an ideal place for a shopping spree, with sizeable discounts available on jewellery, cosmetics, alcohol and Lladro porcelain because of its VAT-free status.

But the real joys of Gibraltar are to be discovered away from the main town, in the backstreets dotted with magnificent colonial buildings and Moroccan corner shops selling fat dates and leather slippers. And then there is the Upper Rock Nature Reserve, which affords access to the Rock's most famous residents – the monkeys – as well as historical sights and unbeatable views over the Straits.

You need to show your passport on entering and leaving Gibraltar. Border formalities are less protracted than they used to be, but motorists may be better off parking in La Linea on the Spanish side. On Sundays, many shops and sights are closed and the cable car does not operate.

BEACHES

Gibraltar's beaches combine Mediterranean sunshine and warm clear waters with the beach umbrella culture of a British seaside town. Catalan Bay and Sandy Bay are popular with young families and get very busy during school holidays. Eastern Beach is favoured by teens, while the less attractive Western Beach, opposite the airport, catches the last of the evening sun.

THINGS TO SEE & DO

A blanket charge is made to enter any part of the Upper Rock Nature Reserve, which includes many of Gibraltar's chief attractions (including the Great Siege Tunnels, the Mediterranean Steps, the Moorish Castle and St Michael's Cave). The reserve is open 09.30–19.15 in the summer and 09.30–17.30 in the winter, and is well worth a visit in its own right for the stunning views across the Straits to the Riff Mountains in Morocco. It is also a paradise for bird-lovers: more than 200 species have been spotted here on their annual migratory routes.

Alameda Botanical Gardens

Gibraltar's botanical gardens are one of its unsung treasures, and host to an impressive collection of plants from Mediterranean climatic zones around the world.

ⓐ Red Sands Road ⓣ 41235 ⓦ www.gibraltargardens.gi ⓛ 08.00–sunset ❶ No admission charge

The Apes' Den

Halfway up the Rock are the famous Barbary macaques – in actual fact tailless monkeys, and the only group of wild primates remaining in Europe. It is said that as long as they are here, Gibraltar will remain British. Although they are wild, they are bold enough to climb on tourists and have been known to make off with cameras etc., so hang on carefully to your belongings. Don't feed them, even if your taxi driver encourages you to. ⓐ Upper Rock Nature Reserve ❶ 74950 (Gibraltar Tourist Board) ❷ 09.30–19.15 summer, 09.30–17.30 winter

The Cable Car

Enjoy spectacular views as you climb to the top of the Rock in this 8-minute cable-car journey.
ⓐ Grand Parade ❶ 77826 ❷ 09.30–17.45

Dolphin watching

Watch the three species of dolphin that swim in the bay from a specially designed glass-bottomed boat. There are occasional sightings of pilot whales too. Reliable excursions are organised year round through:

Dolphin Adventure ⓐ Marina Bay ❶ 50650 or 685 60 82 08 ⓦ www.dolphinadventure.eu
Dolphin World ⓐ Ferry Terminal, Waterport ❶ 677 27 88 45
The Original Dolphin Safari ⓐ 6 The Square, Marina Bay ❶ 71914 or 607 29 04 00 ⓦ www.dolphinsafari.gi

Europa Point

On a clear day you can see all the way to Africa from the southernmost point of the Rock – the 'tip of Europe'.
❶ No admission charge

Gibraltar Crystal Glass Factory

See traditional glass blowing in action in this museum and shop, without any pressure to buy.
ⓐ Grand Casemates Square ❷ 09.00–19.00 Mon–Fri, 09.00–14.00 Sat, closed Sun ❶ No admission charge

The Gibraltar Museum

A visit to Gibraltar's museum provides an invaluable historic insight into the Rock, including artefacts from Phoenician and Neanderthal settlements as well as its more recent past, and a 15-minute film summarising its history. The lower part of the museum also houses

what's claimed to be the best-preserved Moorish bathhouse in Europe.
ⓐ 18/20 Bomb House Lane ❶ 74289 ⓦ www.gib.gi/museum
🕐 10.00–18.00 Mon–Fri, 10.00–14.00 Sat, closed Sun ❶ Admission charge

Great Siege Tunnels

This vast network of tunnels (48 km/29 miles) was blasted into the Rock in 1782 so that British forces could position their cannons at a great height and win the Great Siege. An interesting exhibition shows what it would have been like to be a soldier during the campaign.
ⓐ Hay's Level, Upper Rock 🕐 10.30–17.30 Mon–Sat, closed Sun

Mediterranean Steps

This demanding walk takes you from Jew's Gate (the entrance to the Upper Rock) up to the very top of the Rock, along its southern facade. The steps are poorly maintained, so only attempt this if you are sure-footed and have a good grip on your shoes.
ⓐ Upper Rock Nature Reserve ❶ 74950 (Gibraltar Tourist Board)
🕐 09.30–19.15 (summer); 09.30–17.30 (winter)

🔺 *One of the recreated scenes in the Great Siege Tunnels*

Moorish Castle

Only the Tower of Homage remains of this 8th-century castle, which was erected by Abu'l Hassan when the Moors seized Gibraltar. It was later used by Gibraltarians to take refuge from marauding Turkish pirates who virtually destroyed the town, and remains pockmarked with the cannonball scars of various sieges. The lower castle formerly stretched all the way down to Grand Casemates Square in the town centre.

ⓐ Upper Rock Nature Reserve ① 74950 (Gibraltar Tourist Board)
🕓 09.30–19.15 (summer); 09.30–17.30 (winter)

St Michael's Cave

Filled with stalactites and stalagmites, St Michael's Cave is the largest of the group of caves on Gibraltar, and has played a fundamental role in its chequered history. It was once home to groups of Neolithic people, then used as a hospital during World War II, and now functions as a dramatic backdrop to concerts and fashion shows. Legend has it that there is an underground tunnel from one of the caves that leads under the Straits to Africa.

Evening caving trips to Lower St Michael's Cave can be organised through the Gibraltar Tourist Board with at least three days' notice. The three-hour excursion is challenging, but well worth the effort for the chance to experience Gibraltar's unspoiled stalactite formations and its beautiful underground lake.

ⓐ Upper Rock Nature Reserve ① 74950 (Gibraltar Tourist Board)

Scuba-diving

The sheltered bay of Gibraltar is a good place for beginners, and also has the added attractions of an artificial reef rich in sea life and a whole host of sunken wrecks to explore. Useful contacts include:

Dive Hire Naui Centre ⓐ 36 B/C Waterport Circle, Sheppard's Marina ① 73616 Ⓦ www.divehire.co.uk
Rock Marine ⓐ The Square, Marina Bay ① 73147

TAKING A BREAK

Latino's & Latino's on the Beach £ ❶ One of the most popular restaurants on Grand Casemates Square, with another branch right on Eastern Beach. The menu offers nachos, sandwiches, chilli con carne and hearty salads. ⓐ Grand Casemates Square/Eastern Beach ❶ 47755 (Latino's) or 43555 (Latino's on the Beach)

Maharaja £ ❷ Friendly, low-key Indian restaurant and the best place to sample Britain's official favourite dish – chicken tikka massala. ⓐ 5 Tuckey's Lane ❶ 75233 ❶ 12.30–14.45, 19.00–23.00

The Star Bar £ ❸ Reputedly the oldest pub on the Rock, this friendly little bar just off Main Street is as good a place as any to sample a traditional English fry-up or fish and chips in the sun. ⓐ Parliament Lane ❶ 75924 ❶ 07.30–00.30 Mon–Sat, 10.30–00.30 Sun

🔺 *The rock formations in St Michael's Cave*

Bianca's ££ ❹ Relaxed restaurant overlooking the marina, good for nachos and sangria or a full-blown dinner. All the usual pizzas, meat and fish dishes, as well as a few surprises like banana pizza and steak stuffed with prawns. ⓐ 6/7 Admiral's Walk ⓣ 73379 ⓛ 09.00–late

Café Rojo ££ ❺ Hearty sandwiches and inventive salads, like smoked duck with papaya. The evening menu also offers hot dishes ranging from lamb shoulder to poached salmon. ⓐ 54 Irish Town ⓣ 51738 ⓛ From 10.00 Mon–Fri, closed Sat lunch and Sun

Café Solo ££ ❻ Popular restaurant on the piazza serving modern European dishes with an Italian bias. Excellent duck as well as salads, pastas and pizzas. ⓐ Grand Casemates Square ⓣ 44449 ⓛ Breakfast and dinner

The Clipper ££ ❼ Hearty pub grub and Sunday roasts in a lively atmosphere. International sports events shown on big-screen TVs. ⓐ 78b Irish Town ⓣ 79791 ⓛ 09.30–24.00

Sacarello Coffee & Co ££ ❽ This Gibraltar institution offers light lunches as well as good coffee and delicious home-made cakes. The interior is decorated with local art, which is for sale. ⓐ 57 Irish Town ⓣ 70625 ⓛ 09.00–19.30 Mon–Fri, 09.00–15.00 Sat

Waterfront ££ ❾ Reliable restaurant overlooking Gibraltar's smartest marina, and serving a range of international cuisine from Indian curries to pizza. Wi-fi access is also available. ⓐ Queensway Quay Marina ⓣ 45666 ⓦ www.waterfront.co.gi ⓛ From 08.00

Claus on the Rock £££ ❿ One of Gibraltar's poshest restaurants, overlooking some dazzling boats in the marina. Expect inventive international cuisine of a high standard, together with a good wine list and cocktails. ⓐ Queensway Quay ⓣ 48686 ⓛ 12.00–15.00, 19.30–23.00 Mon–Fri, 19.30–23.00 Sat, closed Sun

Gauchos £££ ⓫ This small restaurant just through a tunnel from Casemates offers delicious Argentinian dishes like *chorizo criolla* (spicy barbecued sausage) and grilled cheese. ⓐ Waterport Casemates ⓣ 59700 ⓛ 19.30–23.00 Mon–Sat, closed Sun

La Mamela £££ ⓬ Upmarket fish restaurant in Gibraltar's 'fishing village'. Eat inside or on the terrace, which has attractive sea views. ⓐ Catalan Bay ⓣ 50540 ⓛ 12.30–15.00, 20.00–23.00 Mon–Sat, 12.00–15.00 Sun

AFTER DARK

Grand Casemates Square ❶ Many of Gibraltar's most popular bars and restaurants are built into the barracks on the north side of this imposing square. Flit between **All's Well**, **Latino's**, **Lord Nelson**, **Salsa Fuego** and **The Tunnel**, and head to wherever looks the liveliest.

The International Casino ⓭ Attached to The Rock Hotel, the casino has a good restaurant and fantastic views across the bay of Gibraltar to mainland Spain on one side and Africa on the other. ⓐ 7 Europa Road ⓣ 76666

Irish Town ❼ There is a string of popular English/Irish-style pubs along this street, which runs parallel to Main Street. **The Clipper** ⓣ 79791, **Corks** and **The Three Owls** are all good bets.

The O'Callaghan Eliott Hotel ⓮ Hosts a popular jazz night every Thursday and some Sundays, with talented visiting musicians. Ask or check the *Gibraltar Chronicle* for details. ⓐ 2 Governor's Parade ⓣ 70500

Vibes ❶ Up some stairs just off Grand Casemates Square, this small disco is the place to go when things quieten down elsewhere. Expect a mix of UK cheese and Spanish summer anthems. ⓐ Linewall Road ⓛ Closed Sun

● *Dine somewhere with a sea view to enjoy the sunset over the Mediterranean*

◒ *The marina at Estepona*

Estepona

The beachfront resort of Estepona is quietly becoming one of the most fashionable places on the western Costas. Its pleasure marina is making glamorous Puerto Banús look to its laurels, while its golf courses attract many well-known international faces. Estepona, though, caters better for young families than the jet set. It makes no sightseeing demands on visitors, but there are few more relaxing places for a stroll than its tidy, palm-lined esplanades. For a drink and a good meal, head for the cafés and restaurants around the jasmine-scented Plaza de las Flores.

This modest, low-rise town spreads along a large expanse of beach. Its economic mainstays once revolved around fishing and citrus growing – the streets in the old quarter all have charming, ceramic name plaques decorated with lemons. Unlike some parts of the Costas, agriculture and fishing have not entirely given way to the demands of tourism, and the town still has an unpretentious and refreshingly Spanish air. Estepona's harbour is a hive of activity when the night's catch is landed on the quaysides. If you get up very early, the fish market by the Puerto Pesquero is a sight to see, but it's mostly over by 07.00. The quiet, flattish coastline is guarded by ancient fortresses, some dating from Roman or Phoenician times. Some distance inland, the road through the Serranía Bermeja climbs through forests where a unique species of fir tree called the *pinsapo* flourishes. From the Refugio de los Reales *mirador* (viewing point), spectacular views extend as far as Gibraltar.

BEACHES

Estepona manages a 21-km (13-mile) stretch of coastline, and proudly waves a Blue Flag (the EU's quality stamp) on several of its beaches. The main strand is the long, sandy **Playa de la Rada**, punctuated by *chiringuitos* (beach bars) and the wooden watchtowers of the lifeguards. **Playa del Cristo**, near the marina, is a delightful oyster-shaped cove of sheltered, gently shelving sand, ideal for children. If you prefer life in the buff, head eastwards for the **Costa Natura**, Spain's oldest naturist resort.

THINGS TO SEE & DO

Golf

Estepona has five local golf courses and several championship links around the smart *urbanisación* of Sotogrande. The superb **Valderrama** course rose to fame when it hosted the Ryder Cup in 1997.

ⓐ 11310 Sotogrande ⓣ 956 79 12 00 ⓦ www.valderrama.com

Polo

For polo, head for Sotogrande, near Estepona, where British and Argentinian teams practise their chukkas during the winter, on Spain's only permanent polo field. Tuition available. ⓐ Santa María Polo
ⓣ 956 61 00 12/61 01 32 ⓦ www.santamariapoloclub.com

Selwo

A successful safari park with over 2,000 exotic species, from giraffes to panthers, in their natural habitat. There are also daily shows.
ⓐ Carretera N340, Km 162.5 ⓣ 902 19 04 82 ⓦ www.selwo.es
❶ Admission charge ⓛ 10.00–18.00 Mon–Sun

TAKING A BREAK

La Gamba £ Simple seafood tapas bar, with fish and some meats.
ⓐ Calle Terraza 25 ⓣ 952 80 56 07 ⓛ Closed Thur and 15 Feb–15 Mar

Gelateria Caffe del Centro £ Coffee, sandwiches and delicious Italian ice creams served in a pretty square with a fountain. ⓐ Plaza Doctor 1
ⓣ 952 80 55 96 ⓛ 11.00–03.00

Chiringuito Rossi ££ This family-friendly *chiringuito* (beach bar) is suitable for a quick snack or a full-blown meal. Great beach views all the way to Gibraltar. ⓐ Paseo Maritimo, opposite Plaza Ortiz ⓣ 952 11 32 99
ⓛ Mar–Oct

● *A fishing boat returning to Estepona*

Meson Casa Orta ££ Lively tapas bar serving traditional Spanish hams and cheeses, as well as *montaditos* (traditional little sandwiches). ⓐ Calle Rocio Jurado 15 ① 952 80 44 38 ● Closed Tues

AFTER DARK

Restaurants
Casa de Mi Abuela ££ Rustic decor and hearty platters of chargrilled meat. ⓐ Calle Caridad 54 ① 952 79 19 67 ● Closed Tues and May

El Rincon Toscano ££ Smart Italian restaurant with wide variety of fish, meat and pasta dishes. ⓐ Calle Real 22–26 ① 952 79 59 14 ● Closed Wed, and Feb and Nov

Marisqueíra El Galiván del Mar £££ Great seafood restaurant in one of the old town's prettiest plazas. ⓐ Plaza Doctor Arce ① 952 80 28 56 ● Closed Tues, and Mon in winter

San Pedro de Alcántara

West of Marbella, the little town of San Pedro nestles on a broad strip of fertile, coastal lowland sheltered by rugged hills. It is less well known than its glitzy neighbours, but Costa del Sol experts recognise a good thing when they see it and many expatriates have chosen to settle here.

San Pedro dates from the 1860s, when it was established as a model farming community with an agricultural training school. Today many of its country estates are prosperous tourist enclaves or golf courses. Much of the town lies inland behind the coastal highway, and it's a fair step down to the beach. There's less nightlife here than in Marbella or Puerto Banús, but its plus points include a well-managed stretch of quiet, clean seafront and three of the most interesting archaeological remains anywhere on the coast. The charming old town centres on the shady Avenida Marqués del Duero, lined with enticing shops and cafés, orange trees and fountains.

BEACHES

There are fantastic watersports facilities at **Bora-Bora Beach**, including waterskiing, motorboats, canoes, rowboats, as well as scuba-diving.
❷ Urbanización Lindavista, Calle Gitanilla

SHOPPING
Street Market Every Thursday there's a lively market near the Sports Pavilion, for those with an eye for a bargain.
Vassiliki This is a popular backwater for local artists. For postcards, pottery, jewellery, ceramics and unique examples of local art, head for the shop called Katoi. ❸ On the Ponti Road, next door to Mythos Taverna ☏ 264 50 31 700

THINGS TO SEE & DO

Archaeological remains

Behind the beach at Las Bovedas lies a Roman bathhouse with a
wood-fired heating system, and a 4th-century basilica with a beautiful
font. Four kilometres (2½ miles) east at Río Verde is a Roman villa
decorated with delightful mosaics showing kitchen utensils.
① 952 78 13 60 ⏱ Free guided tours on Tues, Thur and Sat at noon.
Meet at the tourist office inside the archway which signposts entry into
San Pedro and Marbella, on the Carretera N340, Km 170.5.

🔺 *San Pedro's pretty church*

Cable skiing

Perfect your waterskiing skills on a calm lake, towed along a fixed overhead wire – easier than an erratic, fast-moving boat.
Cable Ski Marbella ⓐ Parque de las Medranas ⓣ 952 78 55 79
ⓦ www.cableskimarbella.com ⓛ 11.00–15.00 and 16.00–21.00

Riding

Call a day ahead to book a horse trek through the countryside at **Lakeview Equestrian Centre**.
ⓐ Urbanización Valle del Sol ⓣ 952 78 69 34 ⓛ Tues–Sun

TAKING A BREAK

La Pesquera de San Pedro £users£ Enjoy sardines barbecued on the seafront or prawns 'pil pil' (in sizzling oil with garlic and chilli) at the local branch of this chain of high-quality fish restaurants. ⓐ Avenida del Mediterraneo, Playa San Pedro de Alcántara ⓣ 952 78 77 21

AFTER DARK

Restaurants

Caruso £users£ Smart, modern restaurant serving popular dishes and adventurous daily specials. ⓐ Calle Andalucía, Local 6 ⓣ 952 78 22 93
ⓛ Dinner only, 19.30–24.00 Mon–Sat

El Gamonal £users£ Some of the best cooking around, in a flower-filled, country setting off the Ronda road. Roast specialities. ⓐ Camino La Quinta ⓣ 952 78 99 21 ⓛ Closed Wed and mid-Jan–mid-Feb

Mesón El Coto £users££ Lovely terrace restaurant high in the hills on the road to Ronda. Attentive service and excellent country dishes and game.
ⓐ Urbanización el Madroñal, Carretera de Ronda ⓣ 952 78 66 88
ⓛ 19.30–00.30

Puerto Banús

Marbella's exclusive and world-famous marina – Puerto Banús – just a short distance to the west, is the playground of the rich and famous, where the international jet set come to shop, socialise and party. It is the Costa del Sol's most celebrated port, filled with a dazzling collection of massive, ostentatious yachts and gin palaces operated by battalions of uniformed crew – very much the place to see and be seen. Behind the port, the 'Golden Mile' to Marbella throbs with nightspots and restaurants. Spot King Fahd's exotic Arabian palace, Mar Mar. Inland, the glitterati villas and exclusive country clubs of Nueva Andalucía stretch back into the hills.

This glamorous complex, named after its designer José Banús, was created in 1968, and its success has spawned a number of rival wannabes up and down the coast. Few, though, can boast the spectacular backdrop of rugged hills, which gives the marina its photogenic setting. A village-like development of eye-catching, pantiled apartments in Spanish and Moorish styles surrounds the waterfront walkways, forming a seamless chain of eating places, bars and boutiques. As the sun sinks below the yardarm, beautiful people strut their stuff on the quaysides before leisurely making their way to the most fashionable nightlife venues.

THINGS TO SEE & DO

Aquarium Puerto Banús
A fascinating place for all the family, this aquarium is housed in an old watchtower at the port. Displays include sharks, stingrays and octopuses.
ⓐ Torre de control ⓣ 952 81 87 67 ⓛ 10.00–13.30, 16.30–19.30 Mon–Sat

Golf
No dedicated golfer should miss out on a visit to the **Marbella Golf and Country Club** (see page 38).

● *The harbour at Puerto Banús is full of gleaming yachts*

AFTER DARK

Restaurants

Azul Marino ££ Superb international fish cuisine served in a smart nautical decor in a magnificent prime waterfront location. ⓐ Muelle Ribera ⓣ 952 81 10 44 ⓦ www.buenas-mesas.com ⓛ 12.00–01.00

Dalli's Pizza and Pasta Factory ££ Pizza and pasta combined in this cheap and cheerful Italian restaurant, with an adjoining café. ⓐ Avda Fontanilla ⓣ 952 81 86 23 ⓛ 19.00–01.00

El Rancho del Puerto ££ Suckling pig and other tasty meats in traditional Spanish and international styles are on offer in this steakhouse. ⓐ Muelle Benabola 4 ⓣ 952 81 62 52

Red Pepper ££ Friendly Greek restaurant right on the quayside. ⓐ Muelle Ribera ⓣ 952 81 21 48 ⓛ 11.00–01.00

Finca Besaya £££ This exclusive, relaxing hideaway is situated in an old avocado farm nestled high in the hills. Accomplished cooking. ⓐ Urb. Río Verde Alto ⓣ 952 86 13 86 ⓛ 19.30–24.00 Tues–Sun ❶ Booking essential; dress smartly

Restaurante Antonio £££ Elegant corner restaurant specialising in seafood, but also offering an extensive selection of delicious meat dishes. ⓐ Muelle Ribera 21 ⓣ 952 81 35 36

Nightlife

Cines Gran Marbella ££ English-language films are shown in this seven-screen complex. ⓐ Paseo de la Ribera ⓣ 952 81 00 77 ⓦ www.cinesgranmarbella.com

Stereo Lounge ££ Modern, chilled out bar with comfy sofas and a marina view. ⓐ Muelle Ribera

Casino £££ Bring plenty of cash for an evening here! ⓐ Hotel H10 Andalucía Plaza ⓣ 952 81 40 00 ⓛ Slot machines from 16.00; casino 19.00–05.00 ❗ Dress smartly and bring your passport

Olivia Valére £££ Celebrated nightclub, and haunt of the rich and famous. Smart restaurant, sushi and piano bars. ⓐ Carretera de Istán, Km 0.8, Nueva Andalucía ⓣ 952 82 88 61 ⓛ Restaurant 21.00–01.00; nightclub 24.00–05.00

Sinatra Bar £££ Rub shoulders with the likes of Antonio Banderas in this laid-back, see-and-be-seen, waterfront bar. ⓐ Muelle Ribera 2

SHOPPING

Boutique 007 Shop here for the latest in beach and club wear. ⓐ Muelle Ribera 4 ⓣ 952 81 13 95

La Cañada Enormous out-of-town shopping mall signposted off the N340 to Marbella, with multi-screen cinema and all the major Spanish high-street stores. ⓛ 10.00–22.00 Mon–Sat

El Corte Inglés This massive department store and supermarket stocks just about everything! ⓐ Ramón Areces, Centro Comercial Costa Marbella, on the outskirts of Puerto Banús ⓣ 952 90 99 90 ⓦ www.elcorteingles.es ⓛ Closed Sun (winter)

Craft market Ideal place to browse for jewellery, bohemian beach-wear and objets d'art, under white tents in the main square.

Kosas Embroidery specialists here will personalise a T-shirt for you while you wait. ⓐ Muelle Ribera J5

Market A large flea market. ⓐ Held around the bullring of Nueva Andalucía ⓛ 09.00–14.00 Sat

Neck & Neck Posh, children's clothes in a street behind the waterfront. ⓐ Muelle Ribera 10A ⓣ 952 81 48 41

🔺 *Fashionable Puerto Banús is fantastic for glamorous shopping*

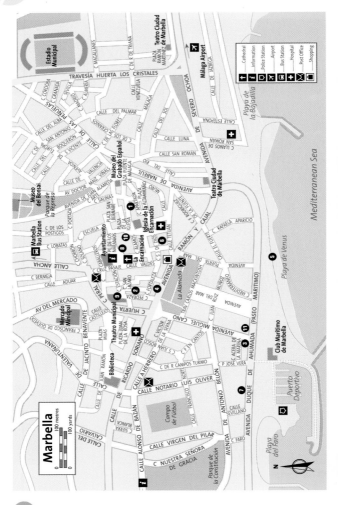

Marbella

Marbella

Glamorous and cosmopolitan yet fiercely traditional, Marbella perfectly blends old with new and is considered by many to be the jewel of the resorts along the Costa del Sol.

The old town (*Casco Antiguo*) has been carefully and sympathetically maintained – a quaint pedestrian district of tiny squares and whitewashed houses smothered in bougainvillea clusters round the postcard-pretty Plaza de los Naranjos, named after its orange trees. By contrast, modern Marbella centres around its designer boutique-lined Avenida Ricardo de Soviano, and the seafront. In the evenings, its smart promenade becomes a catwalk for well-dressed Spanish families.

BEACHES & WATERSPORTS

The Marbella coastline has 26 km (16 miles) of attractive, well-tended sandy beaches. The central beaches stretch either side of the *puerto deportivo* (yacht marina) below elegant, traffic-free promenades. There are plenty of places to lounge beneath a parasol, but many visitors seize the opportunity to enjoy energetic, high-tech watersports of all kinds.

Club Maritimo de Marbella Scuba-diving, sailing and windsurfing near Marbella's yacht harbour. ⓐ Puerto Deportivo ⓣ 952 77 25 04

Happy Divers Marbella Scuba-diving and boat trips. ⓐ Puerto Deportivo ⓣ 952 88 90 00 ⓦ www.happy-divers-marbella.com

Hotel Marbella Club Motorboats, windsurfing, kitesurfing, waterskiing, pedaloes, canoes and catamarans. ⓐ Blvd Principe Alfonso von Hohenlohe ⓣ 952 82 22 11

Hotel Puente Romano Motorboats, windsurfing, kitesurfing, waterskiing, pedaloes, canoes and catamarans. ⓐ Carretera N340, Km 177 ⓣ 952 82 09 00 ⓦ www.puenteromano.com

THINGS TO SEE & DO

Funny Beach

Go-karting, laser games, water-slides, bumper boats (an aquatic version of dodgems), mini-golf, jetskiing and a giant Scalextric.
ⓐ Carretera N340, Km 184 ⓣ 952 82 33 59 ⓦ www.funnybeach.net

Golf

For anyone interested in golf there are many splendid courses in the area immediately around Marbella. So high is the standard of the golfing facilities that numerous top international players come here to practise during the winter, and some have permanent connections with the area. The swankiest clubs are situated mostly to the west in the hills of Nueva Andalucía. Most demand a handicap certificate, and require booking well in advance. Contact the tourist office for details.

Aloha Golf ⓐ Nueva Andalucía ⓦ www.clubdegolfaloha.com
Las Brisas ⓦ www.brisasgolf.com
Marbella Golf and Country Club This exclusive course is on the Málaga side. ⓐ Carretera N340, Km 188 ⓣ 952 83 05 00 ⓦ www.marbellagolf.com
La Quinta ⓦ www.laquintagolf.com

Museo del Bonsai (Bonsai Museum)

The only such venture in Spain, with 300 specimens up to 450 years old, set in attractive Japanese-style gardens.
ⓐ Parque Arroyo de la Represa ⓣ 952 86 29 26 ⓛ 10.30–13.30, 17.00–20.00 (summer); 10.30–13.30, 16.00–19.00 (winter) ⓘ Admission charge

Museo del Grabado Español Contemporáneo (Museum of Contemporary Spanish Engravings)

Important collection of engravings in a former 17th-century hospital near the Arab city walls. It provides a comprehensive overview of Spanish artistic trends since the 19th century, including works by Picasso, Miró and Dalí.
ⓐ Calle Hospital Bazán ⓣ 952 71 57 41 ⓛ 10.00–13.45, 18.00–21.00 Tues–Sat (summer); 10.00–14.00, 17.30–20.30 Tues–Sat (winter) ⓘ Admission charge

🔺 *The breathtaking setting of the Aloha Golf Course*

Teatro Ciudad de Marbella (City Theatre)

A plush venue that attracts an impressive rosta of international operas, concerts and dance shows, as well as plays in Spanish. Ticket prices can be very reasonable.

ⓐ Plaza Ramón Martinez ☎ 952 90 31 59 ❶ Famous names also perform at the grander hotels

EXCURSIONS

Mini cruise

Travel by boat from Marbella to Puerto Banús. The journey takes approximately 30 minutes.

ⓐ Victoria S, Marbella Marina ☎ 952 45 67 50 🕓 Departures from Marbella at regular intervals ❶ Dolphin-watching trips are also available

Ojén

This picturesque mountain village lies about 10 km (6 miles) north of Marbella, high in the hills of the Sierra Blanca. Just beyond the village, in a forested game reserve, is the Refugio de Juanar, a charming hunting-lodge inn (☎ 952 88 10 00 ⓦ www.juanar.com). This makes a good starting point for walks through the hills, where you may catch sight of the rare Iberian ibex, a horned goat-like creature. If you don't feel energetic, just enjoy a good lunch. Ojén is on a bus route from Marbella. Jeep excursions, treks and mountain-bike hire are organised by **Monte Aventura**. Ask your rep, hotel or the tourist office for more information.

ⓐ Oficina de Turismo Rural, Plaza de Andalucía 1, Ojén ☎ 952 88 15 19 ⓦ www.monteaventura.com

TAKING A BREAK

Bar Altamirano £ ❶   Characterful spot on a quiet square near the walls at the back of the old town. Tiled wall plaques promise exotic sea fare: bleaks, saurels, elephant fish. ⓐ Plaza de Altamirano ☎ 952 82 49 32 🕓 13.00–16.00, 20.00–24.00. Closed Wed

El Estrecho £ ❷ A real locals' tapas bar down a narrow alleyway.
ⓐ Calle San Lázaro 12 ① 952 77 00 04 ⓛ Mon–Sat

Bar el Bodegon ££ ❸ Choose from 80 varieties of *montaditos*
(traditional little sandwiches) to enjoy sitting at barrels overlooking the
marina. ⓐ Paseo Maritimo

Cafetería Marbella ££ ❹ A good bet for breakfast or coffee on Marbella's
smartest shopping street, near the shady Alameda Gardens. Plenty of
terrace space. ⓐ Avenida Ramón y Cajal ① 952 86 11 44

AFTER DARK

Restaurants
Palms £ ❺ Beach café specialising in more interesting salads
than most, as well as excellent catch-of-the-day fish dishes.
ⓐ Playa de Venus

El Patio Andaluz £ ❻ A simple but good-value Spanish restaurant set
in a pleasant, cool, flower-filled courtyard. ⓐ Calle San Juan de Dios 4

SHOPPING
Marbella's smartest shopping street is **Ramón y Cajal**. The old
town has lots of crafts and attractive souvenirs on sale. Marbella's
street market takes place by the football stadium on Mondays.
Bravo One of Marbella's best leatherware shops – bags and shoes
galore. ⓐ Ramón y Cajal 5 ① 952 77 32 35
El Camino Traditional flamenco costumes and accessories for
children and adults. ⓐ Calle Estación 2 ① 952 77 50 04
Málaga Plaza Shopping complex with a range of boutiques on
several floors and a café. ⓐ Armengual de la Mota 12
① 952 61 40 40

Restaurante la Axarquía £ ❼ Good-value fish restaurant specialising in paella and whole fish baked in salt. ⓐ Paseo Marítimo ❶ 952 86 36 31 ❶ Closed Wed

Mena ££ ❽ The terrace restaurants on the main square are geared towards tourists, but this little place isn't bad value. Lovely setting in an old house with tables under the orange trees. ⓐ 10 Plaza de los Naranjos ❶ 952 77 15 97 ❶ 11.00–23.00 Mon–Sat

La Pesquera ££ ❾ Highly rated seafood chain with traditional Spanish decor and good *dorado* (red mullet) and lobster. ⓐ Plaza de la Victoria or Paseo Marítimo ❶ 952 76 51 70/86 85 20 ❿ www.lapesquera.com

Restaurante Buenaventura Plaza £££ ❿ A restaurant for a special occasion, strung with fairy lights and situated off a pretty little square in the old town. The inventive menu offers modern takes on traditional Spanish dishes, like lobster with mushroom jam or duck with Málaga wine. ⓐ Plaza de la Iglesia de la Encarnación 5 ❶ 952 85 80 69

Santiago £££ ⓫ A suave but rather expensive seafront restaurant situated near the port. On offer is a splendid array of authentic Andalucían dishes served in a lively and very Spanish atmosphere. ⓐ Paseo Marítimo 5 ❶ 952 77 00 78 ❿ www.restaurantesantiago.com

Nightlife

Most of Marbella's liveliest nightlife centres on Puerto Banús (see pages 33–4), or takes place in various hotels. Dress up, refuel your wallet and head for the cocktail bars of the **Marbella Club** or the **Puente Romano** or to Marbella's chichi Moroccan-themed garden club, **La Notte** (ⓐ Camino de la Cruz ❶ 952 77 76 25 ❶ Closed Sun). There are a few bars around Puerto Deportivo, but for some real action head to **Dreamers**, a popular club that hosts visiting DJs and stays open to 06.00 or 07.00 at weekends. ⓐ Carretera Cádiz Km 175 ❶ 952 81 20 80

Fuengirola

Fuengirola is a lively and popular seaside resort with beautiful beaches, a vibrant nightlife and lots of attractions for all ages. The beach is the centre of activity – day and night. It is lined by one of the longest promenades on the Mediterranean (it takes about two hours to walk from one end to the other). Just behind the palm-lined walkway, the old fishermen's district of Santa Fé has retained its Andalucían character. Its narrow, whitewashed streets contain some of the best restaurants in town, especially around the main square – Plaza de la Constitución – and along Calle Moncayo, nicknamed the 'Street of the Hungry'.

BEACHES

Fuengirola boasts one of the best seafronts of the entire Costa, with over 7 km (4½ miles) of clean, sandy beaches, divided into restaurant-beach strips, each renting out lounge chairs, parasols and pedaloes. The central beaches of Santa Amalia, Castillo and Fuengirola lap the old town to either side of the port, while to the east the sand continues in an unending sweep past the hotel zones of Los Boliches and Torreblanca.

THINGS TO SEE & DO

Boat trips

Daily fishing trips, dolphin-spotting and sunset cruises are all on offer at the marina.
The Dawn Approach ❶ 649 19 41 03 Ⓦ www.dawnapproach.co.uk
Joren Maria II ❶ 952 44 48 81

Fuengirola Zoo

First-class zoo with a simulated rainforest and more than 140 animal species. ⓐ Avda Camilo Jose Cela 6 ❶ 952 66 63 01 ❶ 10.00–20.00, or 24.00 in high season ❶ Admission charge

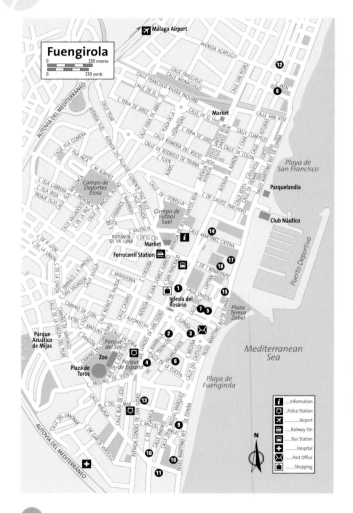

Fuengirola

Parque Acuático de Mijas

Children will love the waterslides, rapids and surf pools at this refreshing water park, just ten minutes by bus from Fuengirola bus station.

ⓐ Carretera N340, Km 209 ☎ 952 46 04 04 🅦 www.aquamijas.com
🕐 From 10.00, Apr–Oct ❶ Admission charge

Parquelandia

Swings, slides, a trampoline, a bouncy castle and mini-karting on the seafront.

ⓐ Puerto Deportivo, Paseo Marítimo ☎ 952 58 12 86

TAKING A BREAK

As Garnichas £ ❶ Informal tapas bar popular with locals, serving great octopus salad and prawns 'pil pil'. ⓐ Calle Larga 4 ☎ 952 19 72 22
🕐 11.00–24.00 Mon–Sun

Café Fresco £ ❷ Excellent English-run restaurant with tasty soups, extensive salad bar, wraps, sandwiches and fresh, mixed juices like carrot, orange and ginger. ⓐ Las Rampas ☎ 635 86 37 95

Cafetería Costa del Sol £ ❸ The place to enjoy breakfast Spanish-style – *churros* dipped into a cup of thick, sticky hot chocolate. A great cure for a hangover! ⓐ Calle Marbella 3 ☎ 952 47 17 09

SHOPPING

Shopping in Fuengirola ranges from cheap souvenir shops to high-class boutiques. For the best bargains, visit the **Tuesday-morning market** – the largest and most colourful market on the Costa del Sol. ⓐ Avenida Jesús Santos Rein 🕐 10.00–15.00. Or try **Centro Comercial Parque Miramar**, a modern shopping centre.
ⓐ Avenida de la Encarnación

Fuengirola's long, clean, sandy beach

AFTER DARK

Restaurants

Meson Galán £ ❹ Deliciously tender *solomillo* (sirloin) and other meaty tapas, along with inexpensive wine that can be enjoyed inside or at barrels on the pavement. ⓐ Calle Marbella 13 ❶ 952 46 64 34 ⓛ Closed Sun

O Mamma Mia £ ❺ Popular, family-orientated Italian restaurant with quick, friendly service. Good value for money. ⓐ Calle de la Cruz 23 ❶ 952 47 32 51

Monopol ££ ❻ Rustic decor, informal atmosphere and unusual, international meats, from 'Zurich veal' to 'Madagascan beef'. ⓐ Calle Palangreros 7 ❶ 952 47 44 48 ⓛ Dinner only, closed Sun and mid-July–mid-Aug

Moochers ££ ❼ English-owned restaurant in the town centre with a roof terrace. Irish beef, seafood, crepes and vegetarian specials, often with a jazz accompaniment. ⓐ Calle de la Cruz 17 ❶ 952 47 71 54 ⓛ 19.00–01.00 ❶ Booking is recommended

Namaste India ££ ❽ Fuengirola's top Indian restaurant. ⓐ Calle Jaen (opposite Hotel Angela) ❶ 952 46 74 10 ⓛ 12.00 to late

Old Swiss House ££ ❾ *Rösti* and fondue, but plenty else too in this pleasant restaurant. ⓐ Marina Nacional 28, one block behind the beach ❶ 952 47 26 06 ⓛ 13.00–15.30, 19.00–24.00; closed Tues

Restaurante Misono ££ ❿ Authentic Japanese 'teppenyaki steakhouse' where meat is cooked at the table on sizzling hot plates. Delicious tempura and sushi are also served, making the lacklustre decor forgivable. ⓐ Corner of Calle Madrid and Héroes de Baler ❶ 952 46 49 32 ⓛ 14.00–16.00, 20.00–24.00 Tues–Sun

El Sultán ££ ⓫   Moroccan specialities in a lavish, Alhambra-like setting. Belly dancing at weekends. ⓐ Héroes de Baler ⓣ 952 46 20 78 ⓛ 3.00–15.45, 19.30–23.45, closed Mon

La Langosta £££ ⓬   Long-established restaurant specialising in lobster, as its name suggests. Mussels in saffron, sole in champagne and beef goulash are other favourites. ⓐ Lape de Vega ⓣ 952 47 50 49 ⓛ 19.00–24.00 Mon–Sat

Nightlife

Hidden away opposite the Old Town Café and down some steps to the harbour is a long row of friendly and inexpensive bars mostly run by expats. Two good bets are English-run **JJ's** (ⓣ 952 58 82 33) and **The Family Bar** (ⓣ 952 46 16 41), a Dutch-run bar and restaurant that hosts live music every night from 20.30. On the front line of bars overlooking the harbour, the German **Ku'Damm Berlin** (ⓐ Puerto Deportivo 12 ⓣ 952 47 28 64) bar and restaurant is another popular venue that serves good food and regularly hosts live music.

The Cotton Club ££ ⓭   Chilled-out atmosphere, the pick of the bunch. Live music most Thursdays. ⓐ Avenida Condes de San Isidro 9

Linekers ££ ⓮   This UK sports bar and fun pub, belonging to Gary's brother Wayne, has cheap beer (happy hour 17.00–19.00), pool tables, English DJs, karaoke and theme nights. ⓐ Puerto Deportivo, Club Náutico ⓣ 952 47 62 85 ⓦ www.linekers-bar.com

Mai Tai ££ ⓯   From 20.00 to midnight is 'Strictly Ballroom' (foxtrot, tango, salsa), then midnight to 07.00 is 'Strictly Clubbing' (soul, disco, rock and house). ⓐ Paseo Marítimo, near Hotel El Puerto ⓘ Admission charge

Ministry ££ ⓰   A welcome break from the euro pop standard, this nightclub is a hit, and often features top names from the international DJs circuit, though it has no connection with London's Ministry of Sound.

ⓐ Paseo Marítimo ⏰ 23.00–dawn Wed–Sat (happy hour 24.00–04.00)
ⓘ Free entry except at weekends

Old Town Café ££ ⓱ A small bar with rustic decor, popular with young Spanish. ⓐ Paseo Marítimo ☎ 952 58 07 39 ⓦ www.oldtown-cafe.com

Video Café ££ ⓲ If clubbing is not your scene but you like to let your hair down, come here after 21.00 for a wild night of cocktails and karaoke. ⓐ Avenida Jacinto Benavente ☎ 952 47 18 66 ⏰ 10.00–02.00 Mon–Sat (happy hour 20.00–22.00)

● *The main focus of most people's holidays is bound to be the beach*

Benalmádena Costa

Benalmádena Costa is a lively, purpose-built holiday resort with a wide variety of entertainment for all the family, good watersports facilities, shops, bars and restaurants appealing to all tastes and budgets. The stunning tiered marina greatly enhances the resort's appeal, and its many bars and nightclubs have made Benalmádena one of southern Spain's hottest nightspots.

Benalmádena is made up of three different districts. Cosmopolitan Benalmádena Costa is the main tourist centre and is focused around three main areas of entertainment – Bonanza Square, 24-Hour Square and the Marina – together offering any number of things to see and do.

Further inland, tucked into the foothills of the Sierra de Mijas, Benalmádena Pueblo is the old part of town – the original Andalucían white village, still full of rural charm. Its sleepy, narrow streets and twisting alleyways of white-painted houses with terracotta-tiled roofs present a complete contrast to the hectic pace of the coastal strip. The main square, Plaza de España, contains the statue that has become the symbol of Benalmádena – a young girl offering water in an upturned shell.

Midway between the Pueblo and the coastline lies the main residential district, called Arroyo de la Miel (meaning 'stream of honey'). It is a busy, fashionable area with hundreds of apartment blocks and many popular restaurants, bars and clubs. Tivoli World, the resort's top children's attraction, is here, and on Fridays the local market provides a good opportunity to buy cheap provisions and local handicrafts.

BEACHES

Benalmádena boasts 9 km (5¹/₂ miles) of beaches to the west of the new marina – some sandy, some shingle, some artificial – but they are all clean and safe for swimming (**Playa Santa Ana** even has a European Blue Flag for cleanliness). **Playa Las Yucas**, between Hotel Torrequebrada and Hotel Costa Azul, is a nudist beach.

THINGS TO SEE & DO

Auditorio de Benalmádena (Benalmádena Auditorium)

Enjoy theatre, music and dance at the town's grand auditorium located next to the Parque de la Paloma. Events run throughout the year, including a festival at the end of July.

ⓐ Avenida Antonio Marchada ☏ 952 44 06 40

Boat trips

Take a boat to see dolphins or go on an organised mini-cruise. Some boat companies combine the trip with a visit to the Sea Life aquarium and a mini-train ride at a special rate. Ask your holiday representative for details.

Castillo Bil-Bil

You'll spot this eye-catching crenellated Moorish building in bright reddish-pink towards the western end of the seafront. Formerly a private house, it has been converted into a gallery for temporary exhibitions. It is decorated with tiles and Arabic bas-reliefs.

ⓐ Avda Antonio Machado 78 ☏ 952 44 43 20 ◷ 10.00–13.00, 15.00–20.00 ❶ Admission charge

🔺 *Puerto Deportivo*

Golf

Benalmádena's challenging 18-hole **Torrequebrada Golf Course** (not far from town in the hills) is reputed to be a 'thinking person's course'.
ⓐ Carretera N340, Km 220 Urb. Torrequebrada ⓣ 952 44 27 42

Horse trekking

Trekking in the hills on a half-day guided excursion, ending with a barbecue back at the riding school. There's a restaurant and children's play area too. **Club Hípico de Benalmádena.**
ⓐ Finca Villa Vieja, Urb. Torrequebrada Norte ⓣ 952 56 84 84
ⓦ www.clubhipico.com

Motomercado

Explore the region by bike or scooter.
ⓐ Avenida de Alay ⓣ 952 44 11 31 ⓦ www.rentabike.org

Museo de Cultura Precolombina (Pre-Columbus Museum)

Charming little museum in the old village with an interesting collection of pre-Conquest South American artefacts and local antiquities.
ⓐ Avenida Juan Luis Peralta 49 ⓣ 952 44 85 93 ⓦ www.sealife.es
ⓛ 09.30–13.30, 18.00–20.00 Tues–Sat (summer); 17.00–19.00 (winter)
ⓘ Admission charge

Puerto Deportivo

Looking more like a giant wedding cake than a marina, the Puerto Deportivo complex, with its countless open-air bars, restaurants and clubs, really comes to life at night. There is even underwater lighting.

Sea Life Acuario (Aquarium)

A small but excellent aquarium with walk-through water-tunnel, touch-tanks and feeding demonstrations.
ⓐ Puerto Deportivo ⓣ 952 56 01 50 ⓛ 10.00–24.00
ⓘ Admission charge

SHOPPING

Andycraft Ethnic imports from Southeast Asia. ⓐ Dársena de Levante, Local 7, Puerto Deportivo ⓣ 952 57 41 53

La Artesanía Española Spanish handicrafts, including ceramics, candles and olive wood. ⓐ 12 Avda Antonio Machado

Artesanía Piel Interesting leather goods. ⓐ Puerto Deportivo

La Maison en Fleur Souvenirs and presents, including tasteful flower bouquets in silk and paper. ⓐ Dársena de Levante, Local Puerto Deportivo A12 ⓣ 952 56 02 99

Selwo Marina

Aquatic wildlife park housing dolphins, penguins and sea lions, as well as a 3D cinema and snake house.

ⓐ Parque de Paloma, Benalmádena ⓣ 952 19 04 82 ⓛ Closed mid-Dec–mid-Feb ❶ Admission charge

Teleférico (Cable car)

A 15-minute ride to the mountain summit, from where you can walk down.

ⓐ Arroyo de la Miel, near Tivoli ⓣ 952 57 50 38 ⓛ 10.30–01.00 (summer); 10.30–21.30 (winter)

Tivoli World

Theme park with world-class rides, Wild West entertainment, and flamenco shows.

ⓐ Arroyo de la Miel ⓣ 952 57 70 16 ⓦ www.tivoli.es

ⓛ Eves May–Sept, until 02.00 in high season; restricted hours Sept–Apr

❶ Entrance fee for children under 1 m (3 ft)

TAKING A BREAK

Café Fresco £ Just like its sister-establishment in Fuengirola, this English-run café sells excellent soups, salads, wraps and zingy fruit and veg smoothies. ⓐ Avenida de la Constitución 17 ⓣ 618 82 68 26

Club de Buceo Los Delfines £ The popular little canteen attached to the diving school by the harbour offers unpretentious, perfectly fresh fish and good tapas. There are tables outside, and friendly service. Excellent value. ⓐ Puerto Deportivo ⓣ 952 44 42 13 ⓛ 13.00–16.30, 20.30–24.00 for food, 08.00–24.00 for drinks

Metro £ Inexpensive pizzas, pastas and ice creams, served indoors or on a terrace overlooking the port. ⓐ Puerto Marina ⓣ 952 44 64 60

AFTER DARK

Restaurants
El Elefante £ Wholesome English home cooking accompanied by various raucous entertainments seven nights a week, including cabaret and hypnotists. ⓐ Benalmádena Plaza ⓣ 952 56 22 46 ⓛ 20.00–01.00

Raffles ££ Friendly English-run restaurant serving good-quality English fare, set near the station opposite a pretty church. ⓐ Plaza de la Iglesia 1 ⓣ 952 56 78 74 ⓛ 11.00–22.00, closed Sat

Restaurante Carretero Puerto ££ Pleasant Spanish fish restaurant with all the traditional dishes, as well as slightly more unusual ones like razor clams and seafood casserole. ⓐ Pueblo Marinero, local E3-4 ⓣ 952 56 41 90 ⓛ 13.00–17.00, 20.00–24.00

Ristorante Pinocho ££ Mid-range Italian with three types of lasagne and good pizzas and ice creams, or you can cross the street to the Cafeteria y Heladeria Pinocho instead. ⓐ Puerto Marina ⓐ 952 44 08 92

Mar de Alboran £££ One of the smartest restaurants in town, near the entrance to the port, offering accomplished modern cooking with a decent wine list. A menu of the day gives you a chance to sample the chef's best efforts. ⓐ Avenida de Alay 5 ⓣ 952 44 64 27 ⓛ Closed Sun eve (summer); closed Sun eve and Mon (winter)

El Mero £££ Sophisticated fish restaurant with a cool terrace overhanging the port. Try the bream baked in salt. **ⓐ** Dársena de Levante, Puerto Marina **ⓣ** 952 44 07 52 **ⓛ** 13.00–01.00

Ventorillo de la Perra £££ A very typical Spanish restaurant. Both local Malagueño cooking and general Spanish fare. **ⓐ** Avenida de la Constitución 115, Arroyo de la Miel **ⓣ** 952 44 19 66 **ⓛ** 13.00–15.00, 19.30–23.30 Tues–Sun

Nightlife

Bar Maracas ££ Samba the night away at this buzzing nightspot. Arrive before midnight as queues can be long. Be warned – dancing on the bar top is a regular occurrence. **ⓐ** Puerto Deportivo

Casino Torrequebrada ££ Take your passport and try your luck at the tables. Not quite as smart as Marbella, but do dress up. **ⓐ** Avenida del Sol **ⓣ** 952 44 60 00 **ⓛ** 21.00–05.00

Joy ££ A popular club in the Marina area, attracting locals and visitors alike. **ⓐ** Puerto Marina **ⓣ** 952 56 34 44 **ⓛ** 23.00–06.00 **ⓘ** Admission charge; Thursday is ladies' night (free entry)

Kiu ££ One of the biggest discos in town, with three DJs and three dance floors, all playing different types of music. **ⓐ** Plaza Solymar (just off 24-Hour Square) **ⓣ** 952 44 05 18 **ⓛ** 23.00–06.30 (until 07.30 Fri and Sat) **ⓘ** Admission charge

Sala de Fiestas Fortuna £££ Hotel Torrequebrada's cabaret act is a spectacular show. **ⓐ** Avenida del Sol **ⓛ** 952 44 60 00 **ⓛ** 10.30–00.30 Tues–Sat **ⓘ** Admission charge includes dinner and entry to the casino

● *Torremolinos is a world-famous resort for sun-worshippers*

Torremolinos

The tourist boom of the 1950s, which made the Costa del Sol a world-famous holiday destination, all began in Torremolinos – a tiny fishing village turned big, brash resort. Few places in southern Spain can offer as many hotels, bars and discos, and, for sun-worshippers, 'Torrie' offers some of the best beaches on the coast.

It once had a reputation for being a downmarket resort, but recently it has shaken off this 'Terrible Torrie' image by smartening up the town and building an elegant beach promenade. By night, the neon-lit streets of the attractive old town throng with life until the early hours.

La Carihuela (the westernmost district of the resort) is a reminder of Torrie's humble beginnings as a simple fishing village. Its atmospheric, whitewashed streets are crammed with restaurants, and fishermen still barbecue silvery sardines on wooden skewers on the beach.

BEACHES

You can find some of the best beaches of the Costa here, notably the two main beaches of **Playamar** and **Bajondillo**. Then there is **Playa de la Carihuela** fringing Torrie's original fishing village to the west, and the quieter **Playa de los Alamos** to the east. All have sunbeds, umbrellas and pedaloes to rent, as well as showers, café-bars and restaurants. At the height of summer, there are often beach volleyball and football competitions. Watersports are available at nearby Benalmádena marina.

THINGS TO SEE & DO

Aquapark
Largest waterpark in Europe, with wave machines, a 'water mountain', and 30 water-slides.

🅐 Carretera de Circunvalación 10 (near Palacio de Congresos)
🛈 952 38 88 88 🕐 10.00–18.00 (May, June, Sept); 10.00–19.00 (July–Aug)
❗ Admission charge

Crocodile Park

Nature park dedicated to 300 crocs, including the largest specimen in Europe.
🅐 Calle Ciba 14 ☎ 952 05 17 82 🅦 www.crocodile-park.com
🕒 10.00–19.00 (July–Sept); 10.00–17.00 (Oct–Apr) ❶ Admission charge

El Ranchito

If you are unable to get to Jerez to see the dancing horses, come here
to this similar but smaller show.
🅐 Senda del Pilar 4 ☎ 952 38 31 40 ❶ Dressage demonstrations each Wed
at 17.45 – book through your hotel

AFTER DARK

Restaurants

La Alcena £ Small but tasty menu of simply cooked meat and fish.
🅐 Doña Maria Barrabino 11 ☎ 952 38 72 02 🕒 Closed Sun

Pepe Carmen £ Paella is the speciality at this friendly, beachside café-
restaurant. 🅐 Playa Camino Los Alamos ☎ 952 37 46 95

Restaurant Chino Sanda £ Cheap, cheerful Chinese restaurant.
🅐 Avenida Lido 6, Nuevo Playamar ☎ 952 38 09 40 🕒 12.00–16.30,
18.30–24.00

Restaurante Nuevo Playamar £ Just next to 'Bar el Guíri' (the
Englishman's bar) is a restaurant that is the complete opposite – very
Spanish. Delicious and reasonably priced fried fish is served either as a
main course or as tapas to a mostly local crowd. 🅐 Avenida del Lido 10
☎ 952 37 16 75 🕒 Closed Sat

Restaurante Casa Paco las Carihuela ££ Established in 1969, this ever-
popular fish restaurant is one of the best in the area and has a buzzing
atmosphere to boot. 🅐 Paseo Maritimo de la Carihuela ☎ 952 05 13 81
🕒 Closed Mon

SHOPPING

Cortefiel It's easy to pick up a bargain in this fashionable clothes store, especially during the summer sales.
ⓐ Avenida Palma de Mallorca ⓣ 952 37 02 12 ⓛ Mon–Sat

Lepanto Superb patisserie. Try the strawberry tartlets or home-made mango ice cream. ⓐ Calle San Miguel 54 ⓣ 952 38 66 29

Licorería San Miguel Great for Spanish wines, brandies and liqueurs. ⓐ Calle San Miguel 43 ⓣ 952 38 33 13 ⓛ Mon–Sat

Frutos £££ A great place for spotting celebrities. ⓐ Carretera N340, Km 228 ⓣ 952 38 14 50 ⓛ Closed Sun eve

A bewildering number of bars and restaurants line La Carihuela's long seafront. Some of the best include **Casa Guaquin** (ⓛ closed Mon) and its neighbour **El Roqueo** (ⓛ closed Tues), at Calle Carmen 35 and 37. **Casa Juan** (ⓣ 952 38 56 56) and **La Jábega** (ⓣ 952 38 63 75) are both on Calle del Mar at 14 and 17.

Nightlife

Palladium £ Regularly packed solid with visitors dancing to the latest rave sounds. ⓐ Avenida Palma de Mallorca 36 ⓣ 952 38 42 89 ⓛ 23.00–06.00 ⓘ Admission charge

Eugenios ££ A long-established disco in 'Torrole', one of the last remaining clubs in the Pueblo Blanco area. ⓐ Calle Case Blanca 22 ⓣ 952 38 11 31

El Luga ££ If dancing's not your thing, try karaoke until the early hours. ⓐ Avenida Manantiales 6 ⓣ 952 37 54 26

Veronia ££ Music ranges from Sevillanas to the latest chart toppers at this lively nightclub near the centre of town. ⓐ Avenida Salvador Allende 10 ⓣ 952 37 24 70 ⓛ 23.00–late

Tarifa

Tarifa has long been popular with windsurfers and kitesurfers, but is fast becoming a major destination for beach lovers as well. The long white strand which stretches all the way from Tarifa's fortified old town to Bolonia is unsurpassed in the region, and the Atlantic water is generally very clear. But what makes Tarifa a standout destination is its laid-back bohemian vibe.

THINGS TO SEE & DO

Dolphin & whale watching

Glass-bottomed boats ply the Straits on the lookout for three different types of dolphin and pilot whales, which are regularly spotted in the area. Try the following:

Turmares Tarifa, which promises a 90 per cent chance of a sighting ⓐ Avenida Alcalde Juan Nuñez 3, local 12 ⓣ 956 68 07 41 or 696 44 83 49 ⓦ www.turmares.com.

Whale Watch España ⓐ Avenida de la Constitución 6 ⓣ 956 62 70 13 or 639 47 65 44 ⓦ www.whalewatchtarifa.net

Windsurfing & kitesurfing

Tarifa is firmly established as the windsurfing capital of Europe, and is hugely popular with kitesurfers too. There are lots of kiteschools offering courses for every level, many of them residential.

Tarifa Max ⓣ 696 55 82 27 ⓦ www.tarifamax.net and **Hot Stick Kite School** ⓣ 956 68 04 19 ⓦ www.hotsticktarifa.com are good places to start. The main windsurfing/kitesurfing season runs from March to November.

TAKING A BREAK

Bossa ££ This small, whitewashed bar is easily found, tucked away to the left of the Puerta de Jerez as you enter the old town. It's a great spot for

⬤ *Kitesurfing thrills at Tarifa*

breakfasts, and also offers wi-fi internet access and happy hour cocktails (17.00–21.00). ⓐ Puerta de Jerez ⓣ 956 68 25 96 ⓛ 10.00–14.00, 17.00–03.00 Mar–Dec

Café Central ££ Just a stone's throw away from the main church, this Tarifa institution is always thronging with people. The restaurant has been running since the 19th century, but the menu is more modern than most. ⓐ Calle Sancho IV El Bravo ⓣ 956 68 05 60 ⓛ 09.00–01.00 daily

100% FUN ££ This chilled-out hotel complex opposite Valdevaqueros Beach includes an excellent Tex-Mex restaurant and chilled-out bar. ⓐ Carretera Cadiz–Málaga km 76 ⓣ 956 68 03 30 ⓦ www.100x100fun.com ⓛ Lunch and dinner, closed Nov–Feb

AFTER DARK

La Vaca Loco ££ There are no starters or puddings on offer at this *churrascaria* (steakhouse): the meaty business is its raison d'être. All dishes come with potatoes and salads and the meat is absolutely delicious, especially the *secreto Iberico*. Reservations are not taken. ⓐ Calle de Cervantes 6 ⓛ 18.30–02.00 Mon–Sat, 12.00–02.00 Sun

Mandrágora ££ Cute little Moroccan restaurant tucked away behind the church in Tarifa's old town, with expertly cooked tajines and couscous, as well as more unusual specialities like *berejenas bereber* (aubergines stewed with spices). No reservations, so arrive early. ⓐ Independencia 3 ⓣ 956 681 291 ⓛ 19.30–24.00 Mon–Sat, closed mid-Dec to Mar

Taco Way & Soul Café ££ Two separate establishments which merge into one, and attract a bohemian crowd for their fresh mint *mojitos* and Spanish dance music. ⓐ Calle Satissima Trinidad ⓛ **Taco Way** from 20.00, **Soul Café** from 21.30, closed Nov–Mar

● *The Roman remains at Bolonia (see page 64)*

Bolonia

About 15 km (9 miles) north of Tarifa, Bolonia is a minute village that comes alive in the summer, when locals flock to its pristine beach to sunbathe. In the winter it has a desolate feel, but is still beautiful for walks into the wooded sand dunes or to explore the ruins of a Roman amphitheatre across the road. At the time of writing, there were plans to develop the ruins as a formal museum attraction.

TAKING A BREAK

Chiringuito Bar La Duna £ Simple beachfront restaurant with the freshest of fish and fantastic views from the pretty terrace all the way to Africa. Try the *choco en su tinta* (small squid in its own ink). ⓐ Playa Bolonia s/n ⓣ 669 456 707 ⓛ Lunch Mar–Oct, lunch and dinner July and Aug

Chiringuito Los Tronces £ Just next door, this super-friendly beach restaurant is run along very similar lines and offers *pez espada* (swordfish) as its house speciality. ⓐ Playa Bolonia s/n ⓣ 956 68 85 33 ⓛ 12.00–24.00 mid-Mar–Nov

Zahara de los Atunes

Until a few years ago, Zahara de los Atunes was the undiscovered secret of this stretch of coast, largely thanks to the fact that it is only accessed via a long curving road off the main Cadiz–Algeciras thoroughfare. These days the village is starting to attract attention – and the inevitable new housing developments that come with it – but it still functions primarily as a centre for tuna fishing (hence the name) and retains much of its old-world charm. The beach here is white, sandy and clean, and there is no shortage of tempting restaurants, while the sleepy town itself is dominated by the ruins of the Castillo de las Amadrabas, built in the 15th century for protection against pirates and later used by fishermen to store their equipment.

● *Perfect white sand at Zahara de los Atunes*

TAKING A BREAK

Pericayo ££ Tucked away up a quiet street, and hung with cured hams and dried peppers, this long-established restaurant offers a piece of old-fashioned Spain. The meat and fish are both excellent, or you could try both at once with the house speciality of *solomillo Ibérico a la anchoa* (steak with anchovies). ⓐ Calle Illustre Fregona 7 ⓣ 956 43 93 15 ⓛ Lunch and dinner (Easter–Sept)

El Refugio ££ This informal restaurant specialises in homemade regional cuisine, served on a shady terrace with views to the sea. The *tortillitas de camerones casares* (shrimp fritters) and the *guisos zahareños* (stews) are especially popular. ⓐ Curvita 10 ⓣ 685 10 93 70 ⓛ Lunch and dinner

Restaurant La Atarraya ££ Friendly restaurant with rustic stone walls and wooden beams on the ceilings, specialising in seafood. The *pescado a la sal* (fish baked whole in salt) is particularly good. Eat inside or under a shaded canopy overlooking the street. ⓐ Avenida de Playa s/n ⓣ 956 43 95 76 ⓛ 10.00–00.30

AFTER DARK

In the summer months, the beachfront is busy with *chiringuito* restaurants that turn into lively bars at night, and the **Discoteca los Tarujos** (**££**) opens inside the ruined castle walls. For an evening drink in a more formal atmosphere, head to **Hotel Gran Sol** (**£££**).

▶ *The cathedral at Málaga*

EXCURSIONS
Out & about

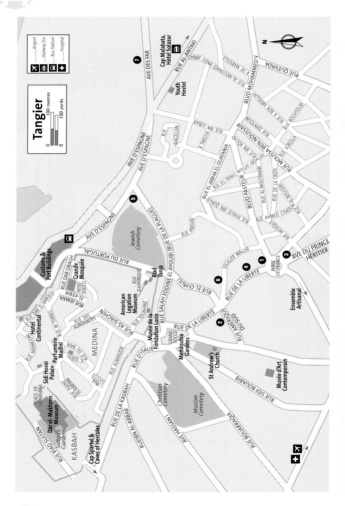

Tangier

0 ___ 100 metres
0 ___ 100 yards

Airport
Railway Stn
Bus Station
Hospital

Ave Dès Far
Cap Malabata, Hotel Solazur
Rue Al-Antaki
Rue Quevada
Blvd Mohammed V
Youth Hostel

Ave D'Espagne
Customs & Port Buildings
Grande Mosquée
Rue du Portugal
Jewish Cemetery
Rue de la Plage
Riad Tanja
Rue Amouja
Escalier Waller
Ave du Prince Héritier
Place de France
Rue de la Liberté
Ensemble Artisanal

Hotel Continental
American Legation Museum
Musée de la Fondation Lorin
Medina
Parfumerie Madini
Sidi Hosni Palace
Dar el-Makhzen Museum
Sultan's Gardens
Kasbah
Cap Spartel & Caves of Hercules
Rue d'Italie
Rue de la Kasbah
Christian Cemetery
Muslim Cemetery
St Andrew's Church
Meidouba Gardens
Musée d'Art Contemporain
Rue Sidi Bouabid
Rue Bouaraqaia
Ave Hassani

68

Tangier

A city with a bohemian past and the grandeur of a bygone era, Tangier, its lustre now slightly faded, remains a fascinating place to explore. Bustling and exciting, even quite seedy in parts, it is certainly not for the faint of heart.

In Tangier's heyday of the first half of the 20th century, residents were famous for their hell-raising antics and sense of fun. The city was well known as a place of cosmopolitan charm where the expatriate good life was lived to the full.

In this jet-setting time, anything went and it was said there was nothing one could not buy in its smoky bars and seedy souks. Artists and writers such as Beat poets Jack Kerouac and Allen Ginsberg flocked from America and Europe, drawn to the bohemian lifestyle. It was also a haven for the stylish and affluent 'Mediterranean set', where film stars casually rubbed shoulders with the criminal underworld and other unsavoury types.

Today's Tangier, a modern port with a large tourist trade, is more calm. Many of the insalubrious night-spots and seedy dens are long gone, sparkling apartment blocks and new resort hotels sprouting daily in their place. Locals good-humouredly call themselves 'Tangerines', after the fruit that has been one of their more famous exports.

As Spain is very close – only 13 km (8 miles) across the Strait of Gibraltar – it acts as the gateway to Morocco for many tourists, who take the short hop over via the ferry (just over an hour). Be particularly careful of pickpockets and hustlers at the port entrance – fake guides will often lure tourists to shops or hotels they are paid a commission to take people to.

BEACHES

If you are not there already (most of the resort hotels are in this area), there is a mediocre town beach near Avenue des Far which continues on from the Avenue d'Espagne. Although the backdrop of white houses

and the mountains is beautiful, the closer views of the busy port area are not very inspiring. Most of the beach is fairly clean, but the western end tends to be the most crowded and consequently the dirtiest. Attach yourself to a beach bar so that you can make use of one of the safer and more private changing cabins. Camel rides and hiring windsurfing equipment are two of the diversions on offer here; another is to watch the locals in their impromptu football matches or macho acrobatic performances on the sand.

If you go via hire car or taxi to the west of the town, there are some pleasant little sandy coves you can access not too far from the city, including **Jews' Beach**, named after the Spanish Jews who arrived on it after fleeing the Inquisition.

THINGS TO SEE & DO

American Legation Museum
A palace before it became the world's first American ambassadorial residence in 1777. Now a US National Monument, it houses an art gallery.
ⓐ Rue d'Amérique ⓣ 039 93 53 17 ⓛ 10.00–13.00, 15.00–17.00 Mon–Fri

🔺 *Tangier Bay*

Cap Malabata, Cap Spartel and the Caves of Hercules

Tangier Bay is guarded by two promontories. To the east, Cap Malabata and its 19th-century lighthouse – which looks somewhat more like a medieval castle – guard the entrance to the Mediterranean, offering views back to Tangier and across to Algeciras in Spain. To the west, the wild and beautiful scenery of Cap Spartel marks the north-western tip of Africa. The beaches in the bay are decent, but can become crowded between July and August. The slightly touristy **Caves of Hercules** are nearby, and provide picturesque glimpses of the Atlantic Ocean. The best way to reach the promontories is by taxi or hire car. Try to arrange a day rate with the taxi driver before embarking.

ⓐ Next to the Mirage Hotel ⓛ 09.00–13.00 & 15.00–18.00
❶ Admission charge

Grand Socco

A large circular market area that was a much livelier place in times past. Now it tends to be a hub of blue buses, taxis and myriad other traffic – automated and human. The market women who sit on the central patch of grass and peddle their wares add considerable colour to the proceedings with their wide-brimmed hats and red-striped cloths. Regeneration work was being done to the square at time of print, so results are yet unknown.

Kasbah

A landmark in the city, with good views of the port. Once the location for the extravagant parties of movie stars and millionaires, this quarter includes luxury villas, as well as a **crafts and antiquities museum** in the 17th-century former Sultanate Palace. The Andalucían gardens are a highlight.

ⓐ North-east of the Medina, follow Rue Ben Raisouli to Place Amrah. The museum is in the Place de la Kasbah ⓣ 039 93 20 97 ⓛ 09.00–12.30 & 15.00–17.30 Wed–Mon; closed Fri afternoon ❶ Admission charge

Musée de la Fondation Lorin

Explore the history of Tangier in this fascinating museum, housed in a former synagogue. Of special interest are the displays that chronicle

some of the city's more notable visitors, including Winston Churchill.

ⓐ 44 Rue Touahine **ⓒ** 11.00–13.00 & 15.30–19.30 Sun–Fri

Parfumerie Madini

This perfumery is famed throughout North Africa for its scents, which are sold much cheaper than brand-name perfumes. It is the place to purchase essential oils, creams and potions – or have a special scent made to measure in front of you.

ⓐ 14 Rue Sebou (in the Medina) **ⓣ** 039 93 43 88

Petit Socco and the Medina

This Medina is smaller than that of most other cities, and it is a bit rough and ready, so keep a tight hold on your belongings. Check out the colourful **Marché des Pauvres (Paupers' Market)** for bargains and the **Ensemble Artisanal** for leather goods and carpets. The central square is the **Petit Socco**, a somewhat seedy square with old cafés and hotels, famous for being the haunt of expats and film stars such as Errol Flynn and Cary Grant and the painter, Henri Matisse. The charm of the place is in its history.

Place de France

This square was once the hub of international intrigue during World War II. The spies may be all gone, but an atmosphere of nostalgic mystery lingers in the Café de Paris (see page 73).

St Andrew's Church

This is a beautiful and elegant little colonial English church. Famous expats – including the eccentric correspondent of *The Times*, Walter Harris, who lived in Morocco from the 1890s until his death in 1933 – are buried in the graveyard.

ⓐ Rue d'Angleterre **ⓒ** 09.30–12.30 & 14.30–18.00

TAKING A BREAK

Café de Paris £ ❶ Another legacy of the colonial occupation.
ⓐ Place de France ⓛ 06.00–23.00

Dean's Bar £ ❷ Built in 1837, this drinking den has played host to
almost every traveller – both famous and not – who has ever passed
through Tangier's city streets. ⓐ 2 Rue Amérique du Sud ⓛ 09.00–23.00

Mix Max £ ❸ Popular fast-food establishment with a better-than-
average menu selection and clientele. ⓐ 6 Avenue du Prince Héritier
ⓛ 12.00–23.00

Pâtisserie La Española £ ❹ Great cakes and pastries suitable for those
seeking an elegant place to rest their feet after a full day of shopping
and sightseeing. ⓐ 97 Rue de la Liberté ⓛ 08.00–22.00

Restaurant Africa £ ❺ A friendly welcome and simple tasty Moroccan
dishes await in this Spanish townhouse. ⓐ 83 Rue Salah Eddine
El Ayoubi ⓣ 039 93 54 36 ⓛ 10.00–23.00

Restaurant Populaire la Saveur de Poisson £ ❻ This unpretentious stall
serves up the best fish in town. Featuring delicious sauces and spicings
that combine the best of local seasonings, it's a great place for a casual
bite or more filling meal. ⓐ 2 Escalier Waller ⓛ 11.00–22.00 Sat–Thur

AFTER DARK

Pasarela ❼ A mass of bars and gardens combine in this large complex
that even features an outdoor swimming pool. Summer brings out a
number of regular live bands of varying quality. ⓐ Avenue des Far
ⓛ 20.00–03.00 Mon–Sat

Sevilla

Sevilla (Seville) is the capital of Andalucia, Spain's fourth city, and one of its most exciting. Majestic, lively and passionately Spanish, it is the home of *Carmen*, *Don Juan* and the cradle of flamenco. As a local saying goes: 'He who hasn't seen Sevilla, has seen no wondrous thing.'

Sevilla is easy to explore on foot, with most of the main sights clustered alongside or near the Guadalquivir river. Be sure to visit the picturesque Santa Cruz district east of the cathedral, with its narrow streets of whitewashed buildings, shaded squares and flower-filled patios, and Triana, across the river, especially popular at night with its countless tapas bars and tiny restaurants. It is here that flamenco is said to have been created, and, for many, Triana is still *the* place in Spain to experience spontaneous flamenco and *sevillanas* dancing.

THINGS TO SEE & DO

Antigua Fábrica de Tabacos (Old Tobacco Factory)

The 18th-century tobacco factory is where the beautiful gypsy Carmen from Bizet's opera worked as a cigar maker, before being stabbed to death by her lover. It is now part of the university and is not open to the public, but the exterior is stunning.

ⓐ Calle San Fernando

Casa de Pilatos (Pilate's House)

Pilate's House is one of Sevilla's finest palaces, dating from the early 1500s and copied from Pontius Pilate's Jerusalem abode by the visiting Marquis of Tarifa. A Renaissance facade conceals typical Moorish courtyard gardens containing classical statues and lovely Mudéjar ceilings.

ⓐ Plaza de Pilatos 1 ❶ 954 22 52 98 ⏱ Ground floor 09.00–19.00 (summer); 09.00–18.00 (winter). First floor 10.00–14.00, 15.00–19.00 (summer); 10.00–14.00, 15.00–18.00 (winter) ❶ Admission charge

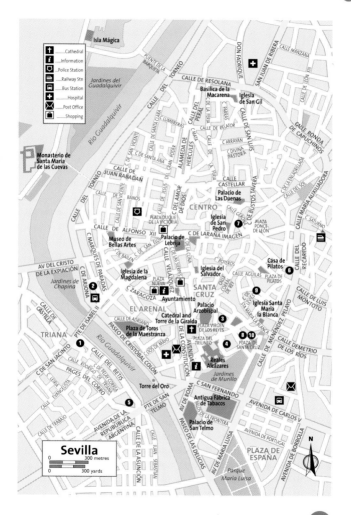

Sevilla

| Cathedral |
| Information |
| Police Station |
| Railway Stn |
| Bus Station |
| Hospital |
| Post Office |
| Shopping |

Isla Mágica

Jardines del Guadalquivir

Monasterio de Santa María de las Cuevas

Rio Guadalquivir

PUENTE DE LA BARQUETA

CALLE DEL TORNEO

CALLE DE RESOLANA

DON FADRIQUE

CALLE DE LEÓN III

CALLE MANZANA

CALLE SAN JUAN DE RIBERA

Basílica de la Macarena

Iglesia de San Gil

CALLE RONDA DE CAPUCHINOS

CALLE DEL PERAL

CALLE DE SANTA CLARA

CALLE DE RELATOR

CALLE DE SAN LUIS

CALLE DE LUMBRERAS

PARRAS

ALAMEDA DE HÉRCULES

CALLE DE LA FERIA

CARRAVÁN

C DIVINA PASTORA

CALLE DE SAN VICENTE

C DE SANTA ANA

CALLE DE JUAN RABADÁN

CALLE CASTELLAR

Palacio de Las Dueñas

CENTRO

CALLE DE BUSTOS TAVERA

PLAZA PONCE DE LEÓN

CALLE MARÍA AUXILIADORA

CALLE DEL SOL

CALLE DE ENMEDIOLLERA

CALLE SATURNO

BAÑOS

CALLE DEL AMOR DE DIOS

PLAZA DUQUE DE LA VICTORIA

Iglesia de San Pedro **7**

CALLE DEL RECAREDO

CALLE DE ALFONSO XII

Museo de Bellas Artes

Palacio de Lebrija

C DE LARAÑA IMAGEN

C DE GERONA

C MARQUÉS DE PARADAS

C DE BAILÉN

CALLE VELÁZQUEZ

C BOTEROS

Iglesia del Salvador

Casa de Pilatos **6**

CALLE DEL RECAREDO

AV DEL CRISTO DE LA EXPIACIÓN

Jardines de Chapina

C DE ARJONA

Iglesia de la Magdalena

PLAZA NUEVA

CALLE SIERPES

CALLE ÁGUILAS

PLAZA DE PILATOS

CALLE DE LUIS MONTOTO

2

C ZARAGOZA

Ayuntamiento

SANTA CRUZ

Iglesia Santa María la Blanca **9**

CALLE DE CASTILLA

TRIANA

PTE DE ISABEL II

CALLE DE ADRIANO

EL ARENAL

Palacio Arzobispal **3**

PLAZA VIRGEN DE LOS REYES

PLAZA DEL TRIUNFO

8 10

CALLE MENÉNDEZ PELAYO

1

CALLE SAN JACINTO

Rio Guadalquivir

PASEO DE CRISTÓBAL COLÓN

Plaza de Toros de la Maestranza

Catedral and Torre de la Giralda

PLAZA DE SANTA CRUZ

CALLE DEMETRIO DE LOS RÍOS

CALLE RODRIGO DE TRIANA

CALLE PAGÉS DEL CORRO

CALLE DE PELAY CORREA

C DOS DE MAYO

AVENIDA DE LA CONSTITUCIÓN

4

Reales Alcázares

CALLE SANTA TERESA

CALLE DE LA BLANCA

CERRA

EVANGELISTA

Torre del Oro

PTE DE SAN TELMO

C SAN FERNANDO

Jardines de Murillo

5

AVENIDA DE LA REPÚBLICA ARGENTINA

CALLE JUAN SEBASTIÁN

Antigua Fábrica de Tabacos

AV DE ROMA

AVENIDA DE CARLOS V

CALLE DE TRABAJO

CALLE DE LA ASUNCIÓN

AVENIDA DE LAS DELICIAS

Palacio de San Telmo

AVENIDA DE PORTUGAL

PLAZA DE ESPAÑA

AV DE MARÍA LUISA

AVENIDA DE BORBOLLA

Parque María Luisa

Sevilla

0 ——— 300 metres
0 ——— 300 yards

N

GETTING ABOUT

Open-top bus tours are a great way to see the city. Buses leave half-hourly from the Torre del Oro by the river, and cover all the main sites. **Sevirama bus tours** ⓐ Torre del Oro ☎ 954 56 06 93 A romantic way to see the sights, hour-long river cruises run daily every 30 minutes from 11.00 to 22.00 from the quayside below the Torre del Oro. Also a night-time cruise (*crucero de noche*) with an on-board fiesta. **Cruceros Turísticos** ⓐ Torre del Oro ☎ 954 21 13 96

Catedral and Torre de la Giralda (Giralda Tower)

This unmissable building is the largest Gothic cathedral in the world and houses a staggering 43 chapels as well as Christopher Colombus' (alleged) tomb. It was originally constructed on the site of a mosque whose only remaining feature is the 70m- (230ft-) high minaret. The views from the top are worth the climb.

ⓐ Plaza Virgen de los Reyes ☎ 957 56 33 21 🕙 11.00–17.00 Mon–Fri, 11.00–16.00 Sat, 14.00–16.00 Sun

Isla Mágica

This fantasy theme park on the Expo 92 exhibition site takes you back four centuries to the discovery of the New World, with spectacular multi-media presentations based on the adventures of the explorers.

ⓐ Pabellón de España, Isla de la Cartuja ☎ 902 16 17 16
ⓦ www.Islamagica.es 🕙 Opening times vary; generally 11.00–23.00 (summer) ❶ Admission charge

Museo de Bellas Artes (Fine Arts Museum)

In a former convent, this houses an important collection of Sevillian baroque masterpieces, including works by Murillo, Zurbarán and Juan de Mesa, and is one of the country's major galleries.

ⓐ Plaza del Museo 9 ☎ 954 22 07 90 🕙 15.00–20.00 Tues, 09.00–20.00 Wed–Sat, 09.00–14.00 Sun ❶ Admission free with EU passport

SHOPPING

The best area for shopping is the Centro, or central zone, which lies north of the cathedral, at the heart of the city, around Plaza Nueva, Plaza Duque de la Victoria and chic, pedestrianised Calle Sierpes. The latter is lined with enticing boutiques of clothes and jewellery and window displays of fans, hats, shawls and flamenco dresses.

Parque María Luisa

Beautifully laid-out gardens close to the Plaza de España. Wander around on foot or in a horse and carriage.

Plaza de España

Constructed for a major exhibition in 1929, this monumental semicircular plaza on the east side of the city is one of Sevilla's most striking public spaces, featuring grandly towered buildings, fountain pools and bright, ceramic tiles representing all of Spain's 51 provinces.

Reales Alcázares (Royal Fortress)

This magnificent 14th-century Arab fortress is one of the best surviving examples of Moorish architecture in Europe and not to be missed. It also has beautiful gardens.

ⓐ Plaza del Triunfo, Puerta del Leon ⓣ 954 22 71 63 ⓛ 10.30–17.00 Tues–Sat, 10.30–13.00 Sun, closed Mon ⓘ Admission charge

Torre del Oro (Golden Tower)

The Moorish 'Golden Tower', built in 1220 to guard the Guadalquivir river, was originally covered in golden tiles and linked to a second 'Silver Tower' by a large chain. Today this impressive 12-sided building houses a small maritime museum.

ⓐ Paseo de Cristóbal Colón ⓣ 954 22 24 19 ⓛ 10.00–14.00 Tues–Fri, 11.00–14.00 Sat and Sun, closed Aug ⓘ Admission charge (free Tues)

AFTER DARK

Restaurants

Kiosko de las Flores £ ❶ A splendid old-fashioned little *freiduría* (fried fish shop) near the Puente Isabel II, specialising in fried fish and clams.
ⓐ Calle Betis ❶ 954 27 45 76 ⓦ www.kioskdelasflores.com

La Mandragora £ ❷ One of very few vegetarian restaurants in town.
ⓐ Calle Albuera 11 ❶ 954 22 01 84 ⓛ 14.00–16.00 Tues–Sat, 21.30–23.30 Thur–Sat, closed Sun, Mon and Aug

Cervecería Giralda ££ ❸ Atmospheric tapas bar in a converted Arab bathhouse, just a stone's throw from the cathedral. ⓐ Calle Mateos Gago 1 ❶ 954 22 74 35 ⓛ Daily

Hostería del Laurel ££ ❹ A lovely old inn with a tiled tapas bar, in the heart of Santa Cruz. ⓐ Plaza de los Venerables 5 ❶ 954 22 02 95
ⓦ www.hosteriadellaurel.com ⓛ Daily

Ox's ££ ❺ A highly regarded *asador* (grill-room) on the Triana riverbank. Basque fish specialities and steaks. ⓐ Calle Betis 61
❶ 954 27 95 85 ⓛ 12.00–17.00, 20.00–24.00 Tues–Sat

Restaurante Becerríta ££ ❻ Sophisticated restaurant and tapas bar next to the Murillo gardens, serving tasty modern versions of traditional Andalucían dishes. Try the cuttlefish in ink, pork in crab sauce, or ox-tail croquettes. ⓐ Calle Recaredo 9 ❶ 954 41 20 57 ⓛ Closed Sun eve and Aug

El Rinconcillo ££ ❼ Dating back to the 17th century and one of the best tapas bars in town. ⓐ Calle Gerona 42 ❶ 954 22 31 83 ⓛ 13.00–16.30, 19.30–24.00, closed last two weeks of July

● *Plaza de España, Sevilla*

La Albahaca £££ ● Set in a typical Andalucían house with terrace, this elegant restaurant is a favourite with Sevillanos. ● Plaza de Santa Cruz 12 ● 954 22 07 14 ● 13.00–16.00, 20.00–24.00 Mon–Sat

Nightlife

Besides its famous tapas bars and *terrazas de verano* (open-air music bars set up temporarily along the waterfront in summer), Sevilla has many other nightspots. Calle Betis (Triana waterfront) livens up as the evening progresses, while the cafés and bars near Santa María la Blanca make an ideal spot for watching the world go by. Some of the flamenco shows on offer in Sevilla are very touristy. Try local bars for these typical *sevillanas* evenings instead.

La Carbonería ££ ● Renowned music bar for flamenco, blues and rock, tucked away in backstreets in former coal merchant's premises. Livens up late; best on Monday and Thursday. ● Calle Levíes 18 ● 954 21 44 60

Los Gallos £££ ● One of the top flamenco shows in town. ● Plaza de Santa Cruz ● 954 21 69 81 ● www.tablaolosgallos.com ● Performances at 20.00 and 23.30 ● Admission charge

Ronda

The old town of Ronda is one of Andalucía's most spectacular and historic towns, famous for its breathtaking scenery, its fine Arab baths and palaces and the oldest bullring in Spain. You will only appreciate its full drama as you enter the town, split in half by a gaping river gorge, El Tajo. The remarkable gorge is spanned by an impressive arched bridge, while tall, whitewashed houses lean from its precipitous brink.

Local legend tells that God, fed up with the constant squabbling of the people of Ronda, sent a huge bolt of lightning down to earth and split the city in two, with the women in one half and the men in the other. This arrangement was so unpopular that they built the bridge across the gorge to reunite the community.

Today, south of the gorge, **La Ciudad** (the old Moorish town) retains its Moorish plan, with many of its fine mansions and the now-Catholic church of Santa María la Mayor, once the town's main mosque. To the north lies El Mercadillo, the new town.

Ronda is the most famous of Andalucía's romantic *pueblos blancos*, the so-called 'white towns' built by the Moors in the 13th century to fend off the harsh rays of the sun. Its stunning location has frequently been used in Hollywood films, including *Carmen* and *For Whom the Bell Tolls*.

There are some excellent walks around Ronda. One without too much climbing is the footpath called Paseo Blas Infante, which begins behind the *Parador* (state-owned hotel housed in an historic building) and leads along the brink of the gorge. An evening stroll along here gives wonderful views. Take your camera.

THINGS TO SEE & DO

Baño Arabes (Moorish baths)
This 13th-century bathhouse is the best-preserved example in Europe, and still functions today.
ⓐ The Riverside ⓣ 952 87 38 89 ⓛ 10.00–13.30 Tues, 09.30–15.00 Wed–Sat, 10.00–14.00 Sun, closed Mon ⓘ Admission charge

⬥ *Ronda and the impressive El Tajo gorge*

La Casa del Rey Moro (Mansion of the Moorish Kings)

This 18th-century mansion overlooking the gorge was built on much older Moorish foundations. Although not open to the public, the house has an ancient underground stairway, which leads right down to the

river through terraced gardens. Cut out of the rock by Christian slaves, these 365 steps guaranteed a water supply to the people of the town, even in times of siege.

ⓐ Cuesta de Santo Domingo 17 ⓣ 952 18 72 00 ⓛ Gardens and stairway 10.00–20.00 (summer); 10.00–19.00 (winter) ⓘ Admission charge

Plaza de Toros (Bullring)

The bullring, built in 1785, is one of the oldest and most beautiful in Spain. It was here that Pedro Romero, the founder of modern bullfighting, evolved today's style of fighting bulls on foot rather than on horseback. Nowadays, the bullring is only used for special fiestas, but the museum is well worth a visit.

ⓐ Calle Virgen de la Paz 15 ⓣ 952 87 41 32 ⓛ 10.00–20.00 ⓘ Admission charge

El Tajo Gorge

Three bridges span the gorge: the Moorish Puente de San Miguel looks over the ancient Arab baths; the Puente Viejo (Old Bridge) was built in 1616, and the not-so-new Puente Nuevo (New Bridge), built in the late 18th century, boasts unforgettable views and is the symbol of Ronda. The gorge, at its highest point, drops over 90 m (300 ft) to the Guadalevin river below, and has a rather bloody past. The architect of the Puente Nuevo fell to his death here while attempting to catch his hat. In the 18th century, injured horses from the bullring were flung over the cliffs. During the Spanish Civil War, over 500 Nationalist prisoners were thrown into the gorge by Republicans.

TAKING A BREAK

Café Alba £ A popular breakfast spot, serving delicious coffee, piping-hot chocolate and *churros* (akin to a doughnut). ⓐ Calle Espinel 44 ⓣ 952 19 09 53

El Corralillo £ This clean, brightly tiled café in a covered passage is a good place to rest your feet midway through a shopping spree. Good *churros*, breakfasts and snacks. ⓐ Calle Espinel 40 ⓣ 952 87 77 33

Doña Pepa ££ Well-respected, family-run restaurant offering traditional local dishes like rabbit, partridge and quail in garlic. Their separate café-bar opposite serves *bocadillos* (sandwiches) and freshly squeezed orange juice. ⓐ Plaza del Socorro 10 ⓣ 952 87 47 77

Parador de Ronda £££ The most perfectly situated hotel in town, overlooking the ravine just next to the Puente Nuevo. The food is also delicious: expect traditional Andalucian favourites like *ajo blanco* (cold garlic soup), roast kid and rabbit. For pudding, try the local speciality *yemas rondenas* (sweet egg yolks). ⓐ Plaza Espana ⓣ 952 87 72 00

AFTER DARK

Restaurants & bars
Bar Las Castañuelas £ A lively local bar where you can enjoy a glass of *fino* (sherry) accompanied by inexpensive, traditional tapas.
ⓐ Calle Jerez 3 ⓣ 952 87 61 78

Peña Flamenco Tobalo ££ Some claim that Ronda (and not Sevilla) is the birthplace of flamenco. Live shows take place in Bar la Plazuela most Fridays. Telephone to check. ⓐ Calle Artesanos ⓣ 952 87 41 77
❶ Admission charge

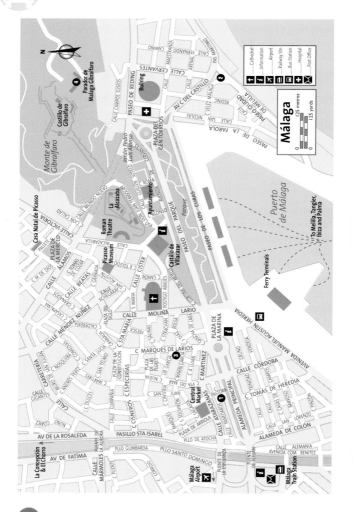

Málaga

Cathedral
Information
Railway Stn
Bus Station
Hospital
Post Office

0   125 metres
0   125 yards

Málaga

Málaga is a bustling seaport, the sprawling capital of the Costa del Sol, the second city of Andalucía and the sixth-biggest city in Spain. You either love it or you hate it, but there is no denying, it is one of the most Spanish of cities – atmospheric and vibrant.

THINGS TO SEE & DO

La Alcazaba (Moorish Fortress)

The remains of an 11th-century Moorish fortress stand in attractive fountain-splashed gardens high above the city. Its terraces afford photogenic vistas of Málaga and its glittering bay.

ⓐ Calle Alcazabilla ① 952 22 00 43 ⓛ 09.30–13.30, 17.00–20.00 Tues–Fri, 10.00–14.00 Sat & Sun ❶ Admission charge

Antequera

The town of Antequera is easily reached by car or public transport from Málaga. It's usually a quiet town, but it livens up on Fridays when its market is in full swing. Most of its monuments are shut on Mondays. The old centre contains an impressive list of monuments, including several large churches, a ruined Arab fortress (Alcazaba) and an archway (Arco de los Gigantes) dating from the 16th century. Both the town hall (Palacio Consistorial) and the museum (Museo Municipal) occupy fine palaces. Antequera's most unusual sights, though, are its dolmen caves, easily found on the approach road from Málaga. These megalithic monuments are believed to be around 4,500 years old.

Castillo de Gibralfaro (Gibralfaro Castle)

One of Málaga's great landmarks, this Moorish castle perched high above the city was built sometime in the early 14th century on the site of an ancient lighthouse. At the foot of the Castillo is a Roman amphitheatre.

ⓐ Monte de Gibralfaro ① 952 22 72 30 ⓛ 09.30–20.00
❶ Joint ticket with La Alcazaba

Cathedral

Málaga's cathedral took more than 350 years to build. The original plans included two towers but the money ran out, so only one was completed, giving rise to the affectionate nickname, La Manquita ('the little one-armed woman').

ⓐ Calle Molina Lario ⓣ 952 21 59 17 ⓛ 10.00–12.45, 16.00–17.30 Mon–Sat, closed to sightseers on Sun ⓘ Admission charge

El Chorro

North of Málaga the River Guadalhorce cuts a dramatic gorge through sheer 30-m (100-ft) cliffs that make irresistible targets for rock-climbers. Above the gorge are the reservoir lakes, which supply most of Málaga's water. The scenery in this craggy area is spectacular, and offers many opportunities for walks and picnics.

Jardín Botánico Histórico de la Concepción

An Englishwoman married to the Marquis of Casa Loring assembled this collection of rare and exotic plants, one of Spain's most important gardens.

ⓐ Carretera de las Pedrizas, Km 166 (off the Antequera road)
ⓣ 952 25 21 48 ⓛ 10.00–19.30 Tues–Sun ⓘ Visits by guided tour only

Picasso Museums

The artist Pablo Picasso was born in Málaga in 1881. His birthplace, the **Casa Natal de Picasso**, contains an exhibition of photographs of Picasso as a child, plus memorabilia and early works.

ⓐ Plaza de la Merced ⓣ 952 06 02 15 ⓛ 10.00–14.00, 17.00–20.00 Mon–Sat, 11.00–14.00 Sun ⓘ Admission free

   In a nearby street, part of the former Museo de Bellas Artes, a 16th-century palace, has been restored to house the excellent **Picasso Museum**, containing around 140 major works. ⓐ Calle San Agustin 8 ⓣ 952 12 76 00 ⓦ www.museopicassomalaga.org ⓘ Admission charge

◔ *Shaded from the blistering sun, the main shopping street in Málaga*

El Torcal

South of Antequera lies a weird wonderland of eroded limestone outcrops. This spectacular natural park is colonised by rare plants and birds of prey. The strange formations are best seen towards sundown, when the shadows are sharpest. For more information, contact the park information centre: **Centro de Visitantes**. ❶ 952 03 13 89 ● 10.00–14.00, 15.00–17.00 (Nov–May); 10.00–14.00, 16.00–18.00 (June–Oct)

TAKING A BREAK

Málaga is famed for its old *bodegas* (wine bars) and tapas bars, which provide a good opportunity to try local delicacies and the sweet local wine, while the smart seafront promenade boasts some of the best fish restaurants in the province.

Antigua Casa del Guardia £ ❶   Atmospheric *bodega* founded in 1840, and lined with barrels. An excellent place to sample some of Málaga's sweet wines. ⓐ Calle Alameda Principal 18 ❶ 952 21 46 80

Antonio Martín £££ ❷   A popular seafront restaurant specialising in seafood. ⓐ Paseo Marítimo ❶ 952 22 73 82

AFTER DARK

Restaurants
Mesón lo Güeno ££ ❸   Elegant Spanish tapas restaurant. ⓐ Calle Marín Garcia 9 ❶ 952 22 30 48 ● Daily for lunch and dinner

Parador de Malaga Gibralfaro ££ ❹   This very special state-owned hotel and restaurant is set high on a wooded hill, and has breathtaking views along the coast. The food is very good, and the set menu is punctuated by tasty *amuses bouches*. ⓐ Castillo del Giralfaro ❶ 952 22 19 02

● *You'll need to refresh yourself after the climb up to the Rock*

Food & drink

From the sophisticated restaurants of Marbella to the simple *chiringuito* bars of the Costa de la Luz, the hearty mountain cooking of the *pueblos blancos* or Gibraltar's traditional English fare, the cuisine of the Rock and its surrounding area is as wide in variety as it is rich in flavours. For centuries Andalucía has been a land of different cultures, and their influences are reflected in the local food – the Phoenician style of salting, the Roman appreciation of olive oils and garlic, and the Arab taste for sweet dishes and exotic fruits and vegetables. The local cuisine is an ensemble of exotic, spicy dishes and bold, sun-drenched Mediterranean flavours unique to southern Spain.

Eating is also a major pastime in Gibraltar and the surrounding areas. Locals tend to eat late, with wine-fuelled lunches lasting from 13.00 until 17.00 and evening meals kicking off after 20.30. They will often be relatively formal affairs with plenty of courses, but more relaxed meals where everyone shares lots of smaller dishes – *tapas* or *raciones* – are also exceedingly popular.

STARTERS

Two of the region's best-loved starters are chilled soups: *gazpacho andaluz* (made with tomato, garlic, sweet peppers and cucumber) and *ajo blanco* (made from garlic and almonds and served with grapes). In the winter, warm and hearty *potajes* are popular – thick vegetable soups which will often contain chunks of meat.

Other favourite starters include *raciones* of thinly sliced dark-cured *jamon serrano* and triangles of typical Spanish *Manchego* cheese, or mini sandwiches known as *montaditos*. Gibraltar's two home-grown specialities are also worth sharing: delicious *torta de acelga*, a pie made with red chard and whole boiled eggs, and *calentita*, a flat pie of sorts made entirely from chickpea flour and best served with plenty of salt.

MAIN DISHES

Fish: Fresh fish is one of Andalucía's staples. If you are visiting in the summer, don't miss out on barbecued sardines, which are often cooked on an open fire on the beach and usually served with lots of salt and lemon. The daily catch in most coastal towns also includes *bonito* or *atun* (tuna), *rape* (monkfish), *salmonete* (red mullet), *pez espada* (swordfish) and *lenguado* (sole) – which are all delicious pan fried or grilled (*a la plancha*). Also worth trying are *gambas al pil-pil* (prawns sizzling in oil, garlic and chilli), *calamares en su tinta* (squid cooked in its own ink) and of course *paella* – a scrumptious rice dish of meat, tomatoes, peppers, onions and a heap of seafood. But for those keen to embrace Gibraltar's British roots, the novelty of traditional battered cod and mushy peas on a blazing hot summer's day is hard to beat.

● *Gibraltar maintains many British habits, like fish and chips*

🔵 *Casemates Square is well supplied with cafés and bars*

Meat: In inland Spain, a rich, traditional cuisine incorporates the game and wild herbs of the mountains, with hearty meat dishes including *estofado* (meat stew), *fabada* (ham and bean stew), *conejo* (rabbit casserole) and *choto al ajo* (roast kid in garlic sauce). Look out also for *albondigas* (spicy meatballs), *calderetas* (lamb stew with almonds), and one of the most famous Andalucian dishes of all, *raba de toro* (tender oxtail prepared with tomatoes, onions and spices). Food buffs should also sample the many tasty local varieties of sausage and cured ham. *Pata negra* is the most highly prized.

DESSERTS AND SWEETS

Remember to save room for pudding – sweet, gelatinous *tocino de ciel* (flan), sticky *natillas* (cream custards), *yemas del tajo* (sweets based on egg yolks and sugar), *brazo de gitano* (cream-filled pastries) and *piononos* (liqueur-soaked cake). If all that sounds too much, lemon sorbet with cava is a refreshing way to round off a meal – or enjoy delicious fresh fruits like melon, oranges, peaches, grapes and figs.

VEGETARIAN FOOD

Vegetarians will eat well in Gibraltar, where a full range of international cuisine is served. In Andalucía, most menus are geared to meat and fish eaters but usually include a range of salads and vegetable dishes as well. Good bets include *garbanzos con espinacas* (chickpeas with spinach), *judias verdes con salsa de tomate* (green beans with tomato sauces), *pisto de verduras* (ratatouille) and the ubiquitous but delicious *tortilla* (thick omelette with potatoes). The options in Morocco are also pretty decent, with vegetable tajine and couscous top of the list.

Menu decoder

Aceitunas aliñadas Marinated olives

A la plancha Grilled

Albóndigas de pescado Fish cakes

Albóndigas en salsa Meatballs in (usually tomato) sauce

Alioli Garlic-flavoured mayonnaise served as an accompaniment

Bistec or biftek Beef steak; rare is *poco hecho*, medium is *regular* and well done is *muy hecho* (ask for it more well cooked than at home)

Bocadillo The Spanish sandwich, usually made of French-style bread

Caldereta A stew based on fish or lamb

Caldo A soup or broth

Calentita Flat pie made of chickpea flour and best served with lots of salt, a favourite of Gibraltar

Carne Meat; *carne de ternera* is beef; *carne picada* is minced meat; *carne de cerdo* is pork; *carne de cordero* is lamb

Carne/pollo empanada Breaded meat or chicken escalope, either served hot with salad and chips, or cold in a sandwich

Chorizo A cured, dry, red-coloured sausage made from chopped pork, paprika, spices, herbs and garlic

Churros Flour fritters cooked in spiral shapes in very hot fat, best dunked into hot chocolate

Cordero asado Roast lamb flavoured with lemon and white wine

Couscous Ground semolina grains – the dietary staple of Moroccans – traditionally served with a thick meat or vegetable stew

Embutidos charcutería Pork meat preparations including *jamón* (ham), *chorizo* (see left), *salchichones* (sausages) and *morcillas* (black pudding)

Ensalada Salad; the normal restaurant salad is composed of iceberg lettuce, onion and tomato

Ensalada mixta As above, but with extra ingredients, such as boiled egg, tuna fish or asparagus

Escabeche A sauce of fish, meat or vegetables cooked in wine and served cold

Estofado de buey Beef stew made with carrots and turnips, or with potatoes

Fiambre Any type of cold meat such as ham, chorizo, etc

Flan Caramel custard, the national dessert of Spain

Fritura A fry-up, as in *fritura de pescado* – different kinds of fried fish

Gambas Prawns; *gambas a la plancha* are grilled and *gambas pil pil* are fried with garlic and chilli

Gazpacho andaluz Cold soup (originally from Andalucía) made from tomatoes, cucumbers, peppers, garlic and olive oil

Gazpacho manchego (Not to be confused with *gazpacho andaluz*) a hot dish made with meat (chicken or rabbit) and unleavened bread

Habas con jamón Broad beans fried with diced ham

Helado Ice cream

Jamón Ham; *jamón serrano* and *jamón iberico* (far more expensive) are dry cured; cooked ham is *jamón de york*

Langostinos Large prawns

Lenguado Sole

Mariscos Shellfish

Menestra A dish of mixed vegetables cooked separately and combined before serving

Menú del día Set menu for the day at a fixed price; it may include bread, wine and a dessert, but it doesn't usually include coffee

Paella Famous rice dish originally from Valencia but now made all over Spain; *paella valenciana* has chicken and rabbit; *paella de mariscos* is made with seafood; *paella mixta* combines meat and seafood

Pan Bread; *pan de molde* is sliced white bread; wholemeal is *pan integral*

Pincho moruno Spicy chunks of pork on a skewer

Pisto The Spanish version of ratatouille, made with tomato, peppers, onions, garlic, courgettes and aubergines

Salpicón de mariscos Seafood salad

Sopa de ajo Warming winter garlic soup thickened with bread, usually with a poached egg floating in it

Tajine Hearty Moroccan stew usually made with lamb, chicken or vegetables, and cooked very slowly in an earthenware pot

Tarta helada A popular ice-cream cake served as dessert

Torta de acelga Typical Gibraltarian pie filled with red chard and whole boiled eggs

Tortilla de patatas The classic thick omelette made with potatoes and eaten hot or cold; if you want a plain omelette ask for a *tortilla francesa*

Zarzuela de pescado y mariscos A stew made with white fish and shellfish in a tomato, wine and saffron stock

Shopping

Shopping is one of the favourite pastimes for visitors to Gibraltar and the surrounding area, with a huge range of items to buy and places to buy them. In Gibraltar shops tend to follow British opening hours, of 09.00–17.30, rather than Spanish, with a lunchtime siesta.

GIFTS & HANDICRAFTS

The best holiday buys here are local handicrafts, including lace, colourful ceramics and attractive basketwork. You will find plenty of choice in the craft shops of Ronda and other mountain villages. Good buys in Sevilla include embroidered shawls and ceramics.

FASHIONS

Marbella and central Málaga are probably the best places for clothes shopping, with their chic boutiques and fashion stores. For trendy designer boutiques and a glamorous backdrop of

Head for Gibraltar's Main Street for VAT-free shopping

millionaires' yachts, Puerto Banús is every shopper's paradise,
even just for window-shopping. More affordable are Torremolinos'
Calle San Miguel and Gibraltar's Main Street, where you can find
everything from jewellery and cosmetics to leather goods and Lladro
porcelain at VAT-free prices. For some reason, electronics and UK
fashion stores in Gibraltar don't offer the same bargains. The Costa
del Sol is also a good place to buy sports clothing and equipment,
especially at the end of the season.

MARKETS

Bargain hunters will love the hustle and bustle of the local markets.
The best buys are fruit and vegetables, leather goods, ceramics and lace.
Don't forget to barter; this is very normal at markets in Spain and
Morocco, so you won't be offending anyone – it's also great fun. Most
major resorts along the coast have a morning market once a week.
Fuengirola Market (Tues) has the reputation of being the biggest,
cheapest and best.

Children

There is plenty to amuse children in Gibraltar and the surrounding area.
Apart from the obvious pleasures of the beach or the hotel pool, the region
has masses of attractions aimed at youngsters of all ages. Many of the
hotels organise children's programmes of fun, games and outings, and
tourist offices have lists of all the local attractions geared towards children.

ANIMAL MAGIC

There is a whole host of animal-orientated activities along the coast
which are fun for children – with the Apes' Den in Gibraltar at the top of
the list (see page 16). The monkeys are bold enough to sit on your
shoulder, but do not feed them as they are wild and can give a nasty nip.
Other wildlife attractions in the region include the Fuengirola Zoo (see
page 43), the Crocodile Park and the spectacular shows of Andalucían
horse dressage at El Ranchito, both near Torremolinos (see page 58).

BOAT TRIPS

Older children will relish the idea of a boat excursion to explore the
coastline. Most resorts offer trips, and many include opportunities for
swimming, diving and snorkelling. Gibraltar also has particularly good
dolphin-spotting trips, often in glass-bottomed boats.

FAMILY RESTAURANTS

Gibraltarians and Spaniards adore children, which means they are
welcome almost everywhere, notably in restaurants (even late at night).
Some have highchairs available and most have children's choices on the
menu. If not, just ask and the restaurant is more than likely to offer child-
sized portions – or go for tapas.

MINI-TRAINS AND CABLE CARS

Most resorts have a mini train, enabling parents to see the sights while
keeping the children happy. Gibraltar also has a popular cable car which
is a fun way of getting to the top of the Rock, and offers splendid views.

SPORTS

When the family has tired of the beach, why not have a quick round of mini-golf, take them horse-riding or try a few circuits of go-karting? Older children may also be interested in kitesurfing and windsurfing, with two-day starter courses offered in windy Tarifa.

TIVOLI WORLD

There are lots of thrills to be had in the Tivoli wonderland, the largest amusement park on the Costa del Sol (see page 53). Children can have a go on their favourite rides like the waltzers, the big wheel, the genuinely scary ghost train and the dodgems, as well as seeing some traditional flamenco, Western or circus shows.

WATER FUN PARKS

A splashing time is guaranteed for all at the Aquapark Torremolinos (see page 57) and the Parque Aquático de Mijas, just outside Fuengirola (see page 45), with a wide variety of activities including the largest water-slide in Europe, wave machines, rapids and a park for small children.

● *Children will love the apes that live in Gibraltar*

Sports & activities

CYCLING

Cycling and mountain biking are excellent ways to enjoy the Andalucían countryside. The tourist board has a guide covering 120 itineraries, with maps, hill profiles, time required and difficulty ratings available from most tourist information offices. Two reliable bike-hire shops are:

Motomercado ⓐ Avda Jesús Santos Rein 47, Los Boliches, Fuengirola ⓣ 952 47 25 51 ⓦ www.rentabike.org; and **Xtrem Bike** ⓐ Las Mercedes 14, Torremolinos ⓣ 952 38 06 91

GOLF

The Costa del Sol is often called the Costa del Golf, and not without reason. With 40-plus courses within just 120 km (75 miles) of coastline, it is Europe's number-one winter golf destination, with some of the finest courses in the world. Most courses demand a handicap certificate, and in high season (Jan–May, Sept–Nov) book tee-times well in advance.

La Dama de Noche A 9-hole course, offers floodlit golf, enabling tee off as late as 22.00 ⓐ Camino del Angel, Marbella ⓣ 952 81 81 50

Los Arqueros Golf Founded by world champion Manuel Pinero – tuition at all levels. ⓐ Carretera de Ronda, Km 42.9 ⓣ 952 78 46 00

Marbella Golf and Country Club ⓐ Carretera N340, Km 187 ⓣ 952 83 05 00

Mijas Golf ⓐ Carretera Coín, Km 3 ⓣ 952 47 68 43

Sotogrande ⓐ Carretera N340, Km 130 ⓣ 956 78 50 14

Valderrama Setting of the 1997 Ryder Cup. ⓐ Carretera N340, Km 132 ⓣ 956 79 12 00

HORSE RIDING

Centro Hípico Hoppla near Fuengirola offers horse rental and excursions. ⓐ Calle Enterrios 49, Mijas Costa ⓣ 952 11 90 74

Lakeview Equestrian Centre in San Pedro organises treks in the countryside. ⓐ Urbanización Valle del Sol, San Pedro ⓣ 952 78 69 34

JEEP SAFARIS

Discover rural Spain by jeep with **Marbella Rangers** ☎ 952 83 30 82 or **Niza Cars** of Torremolinos ☎ 952 38 14 48

SCUBA-DIVING

The sheltered bay of Gibraltar is a good place for beginners, and also has the added attractions of an artificial reef rich in sea life and a whole host of sunken shipwrecks to explore. Useful contacts include: **Aquatech** in Fuengirola ☎ 952 66 03 27; and **Club de Buceo** in Benalmádena ☎ 952 56 23 65

SKIING

Northeast of Málaga, the Sierra Nevada is the most southerly ski region in Europe and one of the highest. Its most popular ski resort is just 31 km (19 miles) from the city of Granada. **Solynieve** ☎ 958 24 91 00 ⓦ www.skireport.com/spain for ski reports

WATERSKIING

Waterskiing is available from most marinas and also at **Funny Beach**, the watersports centre just east of Marbella ⓐ Carretera N340, Km 184 ☎ 952 82 33 59 ⓦ www.funnybeach.net. Alternatively, **Cable Ski Marbella** offers the perfect way for beginners to learn – in calm waters and without a boat! Instead, an overhead cable takes you round an 800-m (½-mile) circuit ⓐ Guadalmina Alta, Parque de las Madrana, 29 670 Pedro de Alcantera ☎ 952 78 55 79 ⓦ www.marbellacableski.com

WINDSURFING & KITESURFING

Tarifa has long been known as the windsurfing capital of Europe, but it has more recently established itself as the continent's top destination for kitesurfing as well. In good wind conditions in the summer, it isn't unusual to count more than 300 kites over the sea. **Tarifa Max** ☎ 696 55 82 27 ⓦ www.tarifamax.net and **Hot Stick Kite School** ☎ 956 68 04 19 ⓦ www.hotsticktarifa.com are good places to start. The main windsurfing/kitesurfing season runs from March to November.

Festivals & events

FESTIVALS

Every town in Spain has a *feria* (festival) to celebrate their patron saint's day, and these festivals usually involve lively parades, music, dancing, food, wine, street processions and sometimes bullfights, funfairs and circuses. At night, vast paellas are cooked over an open fire and the celebrations continue with singing, flamenco and fireworks. The largest and most spectacular is in Málaga in August. For more details consult
ⓦ www.andalucia.com/festival

Gibraltar hosts a small *feria*, and joins in with the one just across the border in La Linea for the last two weeks of July. Its other big event is 'National Day' (10 September), when the streets are decked with Gibraltar and Union flags and everybody wears red and white.

FLAMENCO

Flamenco originates from Andalucía, with Moorish origins that can be heard in the dance's wailing chants. There are two types of flamenco – the slow, emotional *Cante Jondo* (deep song) and the bright, cheerful *Cante Chico* (light song), with rousing melodies and, of course, the wonderful, rhythmic clapping, stamping and castanet playing. With the men in their slim, Córdoban suits and the women in sweeping, ruffled gypsy dresses, the dance offers excitement and colour second to none:

Ali Oli ⓐ Paseo Marítimo, Fuengirola ⓣ 952 19 93 19 ⓛ Fri nights

Los Gallos ⓐ Plaza de Santa Cruz, Sevilla ⓣ 954 21 69 81 ⓛ Nightly at 21.00 and 23.30

Pepe Lopez ⓐ Plaza de la Gamba Alegre, Torremolinos ⓣ 952 38 12 84 ⓛ Mon–Sat nights

Sala Flamenca Donde Maña ⓐ Calle Vicente Blasco, Marbella ⓣ 654 68 55 75 ⓛ Mon–Sat at 23.00

Tablao Cardenal ⓐ Calle Torrijos, Córdoba 10 ⓣ 957 48 31 12 ⓛ Wed–Sun at 22.30

The mesmerising excitement of a flamenco display

⬤ *Colourful boats adorn the beaches*

VIRGEN DEL CARMEN

If you happen to take a holiday on the Costa del Sol on 16 July, you should make an effort to catch this colourful and lively fiesta. Essentially, it's a 'blessing of the waters' ceremony, a reminder that those big holiday resorts were once just simple fishing communities. There are several days of events, which culminate in a splendid procession in which the patron saint of fishermen is carried from the church into the sea. The celebrations take place in several places, but are especially magnificent in **Los Boliches, Fuengirola**.

▶ *It may seem strange to see British bobbies in the Mediterranean*

Accommodation

The following is a brief selection of hotels in the area, graded by approximate price:

£ = budget   ££ = mid-range   £££ = expensive

BENALMÁDENA COSTA

Sunset Beach Club ££ Good-value holiday hotel set away from the Puerto Deportivo, close to a good beach on the far side of Castillo Bil-Bil.
ⓐ Avenida del Sol 5, Benalmádena Costa ⓣ 952 57 94 00
ⓦ www.sunsetbeachclub.com

BOLONIA

Hostal Bellavista £ Low-key, family-run hotel with great sea views.
ⓐ Bellavista 21, Bolonia ⓣ 956 68 85 53

ESTEPONA

Hotel Mediterráneo £ Simple 1-star hotel facing the sea and a short walk from Estepona's old town centre. Recommended budget option.
ⓐ Avenida de España 68, Estepona ⓣ 952 79 33 93

FUENGIROLA

Hostal Marbella £ Quaint little family-run hotel in one of the nicest streets in Fuengirola town centre, and a short walk from the beach.
ⓐ Calle Marbella 34, Fuengirola ⓣ 952 664 503
ⓦ www.hostalmarbellainfo.com

GIBRALTAR

Bristol Hotel ££ The entrance to the Bristol is smarter and more spacious than some of its rooms, but they're still not bad value given the hotel's very central location, just off Gibraltar's Main Street. Facilities include a small swimming pool. ⓐ 8/10 Cathedral Square, Gibraltar ⓣ 76800
ⓦ www.bristolhotel.gi

The Rock Hotel £££ A Gibraltar institution with unsurpassed views to Africa, which make up for the ten-minute walk from town. The hotel itself dates back to the 1930s and is still possessed of an old-fashioned feel, as well as a casino and a swimming pool. ⓐ 3 Europa Road, Gibraltar ⓣ 73000 ⓦ www.rockhotelgibraltar.com

MÁLAGA

Hotel NH Málaga ££ This very comfortable modern hotel is well placed for making the most of Málaga's shopping and sightseeing opportunities. ⓐ Avenida Rio Guadalmedina, Málaga ⓣ 952 07 13 23 ⓦ www.nh-hotels.com

MARBELLA

Hotel los Monteros £££ One of Marbella's premier hotels, with a renowned haute cuisine restaurant and its own private beach club. ⓐ Carretera Cádiz km 187, Marbella ⓣ 952 77 17 00 ⓦ www.monteros.com

PUERTO BANÚS

Hotel H10 Andalucía Plaza £££ Plush 4-star hotel with swimming pool, Turkish baths, casino and two different restaurants in one of the most upmarket districts on the Costa del Sol. ⓐ Urbanización Nueva Andalucía, Puerto Banús ⓣ 952 24 32 42 ⓦ www.h10hotels.com

RONDA

Hotel Royal £ Cheap and cheerful *pensión* (small, family-run hotel) 150 m (164 yds) from Ronda's bullring, with clean rooms and friendly staff. ⓐ Virgen de la Paz 42, Ronda ⓣ 952 87 11 41

SAN PEDRO DE ALCÁNTARA

Hotel Alcotán £ Traditional Spanish *pensión* with clean rooms and friendly staff. ⓐ Urbanización Cortijo Blanco, San Pedro de Alcántara ⓣ 952 78 05 38

SEVILLA

Hotel Béquer ££ Comfortable hotel ten minutes from Sevilla's Giralda, with its own rooftop swimming pool. It doesn't feel quite as plush as its four stars suggest, but still comes highly recommended. ⓐ Calle Reyes Católicos 4, Sevilla ⓣ 954 228 900 ⓦ www.hotelbequer.com

TARIFA

100% FUN ££ Just across the road from the beautiful Valdevaqueros beach, 100% FUN is a good bet for families, with well-priced chalets set about tended gardens. Facilities include a swimming pool, an excellent Tex-Mex restaurant and chilled-out bar, and the hotel is happy to organise kitesurfing, boogie-board hire and other activities. ⓐ Carretera Cadiz–Málaga km 76, Tarifa ⓣ 956 68 03 30 ⓦ www.100x100fun.com ⓛ Closed Nov–Feb

TORREMOLINOS

Hotel Los Jazmines ££ Towerblock hotel with its own swimming pool and gardens, a good walk from Torremolinos town but just across the road from the beach and a number of good *chiringuitos* (beach restaurants/bars). ⓐ Avenida del Lido 6, Torremolinos ⓣ 952 38 50 33 ⓦ www.hotellosjazmines.com

ZAHARA DE LOS ATUNES

Hotel Dona Lola Zahara ££ Excellent-value 3-star hotel with helpful staff and something of a luxury feel. ⓐ Plaza Thomson 1, Zahara de los Atunes ⓣ 956 43 90 09 or 956 43 90 68 ⓦ www.donalolazahara.com

Preparing to go

GETTING THERE

Gibraltar and the surrounding areas are easily reached by plane, with regular flights direct to Gibraltar, Málaga, Sevilla, Jerez and Tangier on British Airways and the Spanish national airline Iberia as well as budget carriers. The low-cost airline Monarch flies from London Luton and other non-London airports around the UK to Gibraltar, Málaga and Jerez. Ryanair covers the routes from London Stansted and Ireland to Málaga, Sevilla and Jerez, whilst easyJet serves Málaga from London Gatwick. The websites Ⓦ www.opodo.co.uk and Ⓦ www.expedia.co.uk are useful for tracking down the cheapest deals.

In July and August, when prices tend to rise considerably, package holidays may offer the best value. If your travelling times are flexible, and you can avoid the school holidays, look for cheap last-minute deals on websites such as Ⓦ www.lastminute.com or in papers like *The Sunday Telegraph*, *The Sunday Times* and *The Mail on Sunday*.

Alternatively, you can travel by ferry, which may work out to be cheaper and more convenient for families taking their own car. At the time of writing there are six crossings from the UK to Spain each week, including a 29-hour trip from Portsmouth to Bilbao with P&O or a 19-hour crossing from Plymouth to Santander with Brittany Ferries. Try Ⓦ www.directferries.co.uk. Another idea if you want to combine a break on the coast with some sightseeing in the Spanish interior is to cross to France by ferry or Eurostar, and travel all the way to Gibraltar by train or car. It is best to go via Madrid and allow three days with a few stops.

British Airways ☎ 0870 850 9850 Ⓦ www.ba.com
easyJet ☎ 0905 821 0905 (premium rate number) Ⓦ www.easyjet.com
Iberia ☎ 0845 6012854 Ⓦ www.iberiaairlines.co.uk
Monarch ☎ 08700 405 040 Ⓦ www.flymonarch.com
Ryanair ☎ 08712 460 000 (Great Britain) or 0818 303 030 (Ireland) Ⓦ www.ryanair.com
Interrail ☎ 08700 841 410 Ⓦ www.interrail.com

INSURANCE

Have you got sufficient cover for your holiday? Check that your policy covers you adequately for loss of possessions and valuables, for activities you might want to try – such as scuba-diving, horse riding, or watersports – and for emergency medical and dental treatment, including flights home if required.

The EHIC card replaces the old E111 form and entitles British citizens to reduced-cost and sometimes free state-provided medical treatment in the EEA. For further information, ring the EHIC enquiries line ☏ 0845 605 0707 or visit ⓦ www.ehicard.org

P&O Ferries ☏ 08705 980 333 ⓦ www.poferries.com
Brittany Ferries ☏ 08709 076 103 ⓦ www.brittany-ferries.co.uk

Many people are aware that air travel emits CO_2, which contributes to climate change. You may be interested in the possibility of lessening the environmental impact of your flight through the charity Climate Care, which offsets your CO_2 by funding environmental projects around the world. Visit ⓦ www.climatecare.org

TOURISM AUTHORITY

For information about Gibraltar, contact the **Gibraltar Information Bureau** ⓐ Arundel Great Court, 179 The Strand, London WC2R 1EH ☏ 020 7836 0777 ⓦ www.gibraltar.gov.uk

The **Spanish National Tourist Office** is at ⓐ 22–23 Manchester Square, London W1M 5AP ☏ 020 7486 8077. It is best to write or visit in person, or you can consult the Spanish National Tourist Office website at ⓦ www.tourspain.co.uk

The **Moroccan National Tourist Board** is at ⓐ 205 Regent Street, London W1B 4HB ☏ 020 7437 0073 ⓦ www.tourism-in-morocco.com

Another useful site dedicated to living and holidaying in southern Spain is Ⓦ www.andalucia.com, whilst Ⓦ www.visitcostadelsol.com deals specifically with the Costa del Sol.

BEFORE YOU LEAVE

It is not necessary to have inoculations to travel in Europe, but make sure you and your family are up to date with the basics, such as tetanus. If you plan to make an excursion to Morocco, it is mandatory to have your tetanus and polio immunisations up to date.

It is also a good idea to pack a well-stocked first-aid kit. Sun lotion can be more expensive than in the UK so it is worth taking a good selection. Take enough of your prescription medicines with you – they may be difficult to obtain in Spain and Morocco. It is also worth having a dental check-up.

ENTRY FORMALITIES

The most important documents you will need are your tickets and your passport. Check well in advance that your passport is up to date and has at least three months left to run. All children, including newborn babies, need their own passport unless they are already included on the passport of the person they are travelling with. It generally takes at least three weeks to process a passport renewal. For the latest information, contact the **Passport Agency** ☏ 0870 521 0410 Ⓦ www.ukpa.gov.uk

For Spain: Citizens of the UK, Ireland, other EU countries, the US, Canada, Australia and New Zealand do not require a visa for stays of up to 90 days. South Africans will need to apply in advance for a Schengen visa which permits entry into Spain and other Schengen countries for 90 days in each six-month period.

For Morocco: British, EU, US, Canadian and Scandinavian passport holders can stay up to 90 days without a visa. Australian, New Zealand and South African passport holders need a visa, which can be obtained at the point of arrival into Morocco. Other nationalities need to obtain a visa from the Moroccan consulate in their country of residence before departure. Israeli nationals are not permitted to enter Morocco at all.

Driving licence: If you are planning to hire a car while you are away, you will also need your UK or international driving licence, which must be carried in the car with you at all times.

MONEY

Currency

Gibraltar uses pounds sterling (£), available in £50, £20, £10 and £5 notes, and £2 and £1 coins. £1 is divided into 100 pence (p), available as 1, 2, 5, 10, 20 and 50 pence coins. Currency from mainland UK is legal tender in Gibraltar, but Gibraltar's currency – which features pictures of monkeys, the Rock and a visibly younger-looking Queen – cannot be used elsewhere, and will attract a lower rate of exchange in Spain and Morocco. Any bank or shop will be happy to swap local currency for mainland UK currency before you leave.

In Spain, the currency is the euro (€), available in 500, 200, 100, 50, 20, 10 and 5 euro notes and 1 and 2 euro coins. It is divided into 100 centimos, which are available as 1, 2, 5, 10, 20 and 50 centimos coins. Many shops do not accept 500 and 200 euro notes because of the risk of counterfeit currency.

The local currency in Morocco is the dirham (MAD). It is divided into 100 centimes, also referred to as francs. The importation or exportation of dirham is prohibited so technically you need to change money on arrival and to change all your dirham when you leave – although in practice some bureaux de change in Gibraltar, Algeciras and Tarifa will do the honours. Notes come in MAD 200, 100, 50, 20 and 10 denominations, and coins comes as MAD 10, 5 and 1. Keep an eye out for counterfeit currency which is occasionally passed on by unofficial money changers.

Banks In Gibraltar banks are open for business 09.00–15.30 Mon–Thur and 09.00–17.00 Fri. They are closed at the weekend. In Andalucía, banks are open 08.30–14.00 Mon–Fri and 08.30–13.00 Sat during the winter. From May to September they do not open on Saturdays.

Exchange bureaux Look out for the sign 'Cambio'; these are generally open seven days a week 10.00–21.00 but hours vary widely. There is one usefully placed at Gibraltar airport, for use by those crossing the frontier.

Credit cards All major credit cards are widely accepted, but cash is preferred for smaller purchases and in more rural areas. Holders of Visa and MasterCard can use the plentiful 24-hour automatic cash dispensers (ATMs), which have instructions in English.

ATMs There are ATMs at all Spanish airports, but it can be a good idea to get hold of some euros from your local bank or the bureau de change at your departure airport to save you the hassle of hunting one down when you arrive.

SAFETY

The safest way to carry large amounts of money is as traveller's cheques (which are refunded in the event that they are lost or stolen) or to withdraw cash directly from your account using ATMs as you go. Most UK banks charge a minimum fee for overseas withdrawals – even in Gibraltar – so it is cheaper to withdraw fewer large amounts than lots of small ones. Before you go, contact your card providers and let them know you will be travelling abroad; otherwise they may assume your card details have been stolen and suspend your account. If you use your debit or credit cards to pay for things directly in Spain, be aware that you may be asked to validate purchases with a signature and your pin code. Many shops also request a passport as proof of identity.

CLIMATE

Gibraltar and the surrounding area is reliably sunny all year round, but it's at its best for beach holidays from the beginning of June to the end of August, when average temperatures range from 28°C (82°F) to 40°C (104°F) and there is very little rainfall. However, inland destinations can be unbearably hot at this time of year: Sevilla clears out in August as the mercury zooms well over 40°C (104°F) without the sea breeze to cool things down. The region is much less busy in spring and autumn, and these can be lovely seasons to visit, with temperatures regularly climbing into the 20s but still cool enough to sightsee and sit out in the sun without burning. The winter sees a bit more rain and will often demand a coat, but the weather is still relatively mild with average temperatures from 8°C (46°F) to 17°C (63°F).

The other factor to take into account is the direction of the wind: in Gibraltar, an easterly wind (*levanter*) usually forces moist sea air up over the Rock so that it forms a cloud that gets 'stuck' on the top (although along the Costa de la Luz, the *levanter* is associated with sunny weather), whilst a westerly wind (*poniente*) often makes it overcast. Ask locals for advice if you are unsure.

Along this stretch of coast you should also pay attention to the force of the wind by checking out the latest conditions on websites like Ⓦ http://tarifa.costasur.com/en/weather.html. A good day in Tarifa is well worth the effort, but a windy day on the beach will leave you feeling pebble-dashed.

BAGGAGE ALLOWANCE

Baggage allowances vary according to the airline, the destination and the class of travel, but most airlines allow each passenger to take one piece of luggage weighing up to 20 kg (44 lb) to be carried in the hold. You are also allowed one item of cabin baggage weighing no more than 5 kg (11 lb), and measuring 55 by 40 by 20 cm (22 × 16 × 8 in). Under current security rules, a woman's handbag counts as the item of cabin baggage and all liquids must be under 100 ml and carried separately in a see-through sealable bag. Large items – surfboards, golf clubs and collapsible wheelchairs – are often charged as extras, and it is a good idea to let the airline know in advance that you want to bring these.

During your stay

AIRPORTS

Gibraltar Airport This tiny airport is well placed for visiting the western edge of the Costa del Sol, and will be even better suited by mid-2008 when a new terminal is constructed with a direct exit to Spain. The expansion plans will also see a boost to the number of flights and services, although most major car-rental companies are already represented. There are always taxis in front of the building to take you into Gibraltar, or just the other side of the border for journeys further afield to the Costa del Sol. A 'Portillo' bus runs from the terminal in La Linea to Málaga, making a number of coastal stops. Estepona is about 30 minutes' drive away and Málaga is just over an hour.

Málaga Airport is located 8 km (5 miles) south-west of Málaga city and is the Costa del Sol's busiest airport by far. All major car-hire companies are represented and taxis are available from just outside the arrivals hall. Public transport connections are also good: buses run every half hour 06.30–23.30 to the main bus terminal in Málaga city, where there are connections to Estepona, Fuengirola, La Linea (for Gibraltar), Mijas and Ronda, and throughout the region. Direct buses run between the airport and Marbella every 45 minutes between 06.15 and 23.45. There is also an excellent train service between Málaga city and Fuengirola, via the airport, Torremolinos and Arroyo de la Miel which operates every 30 minutes (06.45–23.00) and takes 42 minutes in total.

Sevilla Located about 10 km (6 miles) north-west of Sevilla and about three hours' drive from Málaga, this airport is well served by car-hire companies and rail links to Málaga as well as Madrid and Algeciras (just east of Gibraltar).

Jerez Full car-hire facilities and taxis to local destinations are available from Jerez. Daily buses run to Ronda, La Linea (for Gibraltar), Marbella and Málaga – a five-hour journey.

Useful advice on facilities available at all airports in Andalucía is available at ⓦ www.spanish-airport-guide.com

Tangier About 6 km (3½ miles) from Tangier town, with car-hire facilities.

COMMUNICATIONS

Telephones

Public telephones in Gibraltar are easy to use and easy to spot – in the traditional red telephone boxes that have long been associated with mainland UK. All accept coins and some accept cards.

In Spain, public telephones are mounted on posts or in glazed, silver *cabinas telefónicas* (phone booths). They accept coins and/or phone cards which can be purchased at newsstands and *estancos* (tobacconists), and many of them also have a button which you can press for instructions in English. Most have a list of international dialling codes, and useful numbers like the operator (1004) and directory services (1003). Alternatively, most restaurants and bars have a telephone available for public use.

Postal services

Postboxes are bright yellow and can be found at railway stations and post offices (*correos*) as well as dotted around town. Stamps (*sellos*) can be bought from post offices or tobacconists (*estancos*), which display a distinctive red-and-yellow sign and often have weighing facilities too. The postal service itself is renowned for being slow and unreliable, with postcards to Europe taking up to a month to arrive because postboxes are sometimes not emptied for days. For the most reliable service, post letters at the post office itself or use the *certificado* (registered) and *urgente* (express) mail. Main post offices are open 08.30–20.30 Mon–Fri, 09.30–14.00 Sat.

Internet access

Internet cafés are readily available in the big tourist centres but can be hard to find in smaller towns or off the beaten track.

CUSTOMS

Introductions

When you are introduced to friends in Gibraltar or Spain, it is customary for women to offer a kiss on each cheek, and for men to offer a kiss to women or to shake hands with men. But most Spanish people know that this is not customary for all nationalities and will often offer a hand if they know you come from abroad.

Complaints

If you are not happy with a service in Spain, particularly in a restaurant or hotel, you are entitled to ask for the *Libro de Reclamaciones*. This is an official complaints book at the disposal of customers, which is inspected periodically by the local authorities. Only use it for very unsatisfactory affairs or just threaten to use it if you suspect you are being cheated.

DRESS CODES

Dress codes in Gibraltar and Spain are pretty relaxed. Spanish men tend to wear short-sleeved collared shirts or polo shirts, but T-shirts are just as acceptable. Women, meanwhile, have a love affair with lycra, and small, strappy tops are de rigueur for the young – usually teamed with heels and big earrings. Slightly older women go in for tailoring and are a little more covered up, with grooming high on the agenda. Both men and women dress up a bit more in the evening and also to attend church. Topless sunbathing is acceptable on beaches away from town centres, but locals don't take too kindly to tourists wearing beach clothes in town, so be sensitive to this and cover up even if others don't.

In Morocco, dress codes are much more conservative. Men are advised to wear T-shirts and long shorts, whilst women should cover their legs to at least below the knee, as well as their shoulders and cleavage. Low-cut or strappy tops will attract a lot of hassle.

ELECTRICITY

Gibraltar runs on a 240V current, and uses the same rectangular three-pin plug that is standard in mainland UK. The current in Spain and

Morocco is 220V-AC, and two-pin, round-pronged plugs are standard. Adaptors can be found in many hypermarkets, supermarkets and also some electrical stores. If you can, take one with you to be on the safe side. Most hotels and *pensiones* have electric points for hair dryers and shavers in all the bedrooms. If you are considering buying electrical appliances to take home, always check that they will work in your country before you buy.

GETTING AROUND
Car hire & driving

All the major international car-hire companies operate in Gibraltar and Spain, and a few Spanish companies, such as Atesa, are also represented. You can probably negotiate the best deal with an international company from home before you go. There are also fly-drive and other package deals, including car hire. Fly-drive, an option for two or more travellers, can be arranged by travel agents. There are car-hire desks at airports and offices in the large towns. Alternatively, if you wish to hire a car locally for, say, a week or less, you can arrange it with a local travel agent. A car for hire is called a *coche de alquiler* in Spanish. Car-hire prices and conditions vary according to the region and locality.

EMERGENCIES

For urgent police, fire or ambulance assistance in Gibraltar or Spain, call 112. In Morocco, the emergency number for the police is 19 and for fire or ambulance assistance is 15.

Medical emergencies In case of a medical emergency, head to the nearest *Urgencias* – the emergency ward of a hospital or clinic. Gibraltar has a new state-of-the-art hospital at Europort. The Costa del Sol has a hospital with English-speaking staff situated on the main coastal highway (N340) just east of Marbella (Hospital Costa del Sol, Carretera Nacional N340, km 187, Marbella,

Málaga). All cities in Spain have at least one hospital, and most have volunteer interpreters who speak English and occasionally also other languages.

If you need to use your EHIC Card, do not part with the original but hand over a photocopy instead. If you have private travel insurance, make sure you have your policy on you when requesting medical assistance. Depending on the insurance company, you may be expected to pay treatment and be reimbursed at a later date.

For minor emergencies, staff at pharmacies or *farmacias* will be able to suggest remedies for medical problems. They are open 09.30–13.30, 17.00–20.30 Mon–Fri and easily recognised by a large green or red cross. After these times and on Saturdays and Sundays, there will always be a 'duty' chemist open, details of which will be posted on every chemist's window or, in Gibraltar, in the *Gibraltar Chronicle*.

Police

The Gibraltar police operate in exactly the same way (and wear exactly the same uniform) as in mainland UK, with one force responsible for all types of crime. In Spain, there are three types of police: the Guardia Civil, the Policia Nacional and the Policia Local. The Policia Nacional, who wear a blue uniform, are the best to turn to when reporting a crime. When approaching them, remember that it is illegal to be without ID.

Consulates

The British Consulate is at ➌ Plaza Nueva 87, 41001 Sevilla ➊ 954 22 88 74 and ➋ Calle Mauricio Moro Pareto, 2 Málaga ➊ 952 35 23 00. The British consulate in Tangier is at ➌ 9 Rue d'Amerique du Sud ➊ 039 93 69 39.

Visitors driving vehicles from other countries need no special documentation in Spain, but make sure you have all the relevant papers from your country of origin: your driving licence, vehicle registration document and insurance. Your insurance company should be able to arrange an overseas extension of your car insurance. To hire a car in Spain you need show only a current driving licence. When driving from Britain, if you have an old-style green licence you will need to purchase an International Driving Permit, obtained from the RAC or the AA.

Most Spanish motorways are well equipped with an SOS network of telephones, which provide instant access to the emergency services. Ask for *auxilio en carretera*. In Spain, Gibraltar and Morocco, people drive on the right so you must give way to the right. At roundabouts, you should give way to cars already on the roundabout but be extremely careful when on a roundabout yourself: do not expect oncoming cars to stop. Some will disregard you and drive straight on.

The speed limits are 50 km/h (30 mph) in built-up areas; 90–100 km/h (55–60 mph) outside them and 120 km/h (75 mph) on motorways. Seat belts are compulsory in the back and front; motorcyclists must wear crash helmets. Drivers must carry two warning triangles and can be fined by the traffic police for not being equipped with a first-aid kit.

Taxis

These are essential for access to out-of-town nightspots. You can phone from your hotel reception area, walk to a taxi rank, or flag one down as it passes by. A green light in the front window or on top of the roof indicates that the taxi is available for hire. Taxis are always white and have a logo on the doors, which displays their official number. Drivers in Spain rarely speak any English, so learn enough Spanish to explain where you are going and to negotiate the fare. The meter marks up the basic fare; however, supplements may be added for *tarifa nocturna* (night driving), *maletas* (luggage) or *días festivos* (public holidays). If in doubt of the correct price, ask for the *tarifas* (price list).

Public transport

Buses Various private bus companies provide regular links between major resorts and outlying villages, including Portillo, one of the largest, which covers the Costa del Sol (Ⓦ www.ctsa-portillo.com). Buses run frequently (every 20–30 minutes) within and between resorts and are reasonably priced. Board buses at the front, and get off at the rear of the bus. You usually buy your ticket from the driver, or you can buy strips of ten tickets called *bonobus* from *estancos* (tobacconists) and stationers. It is not unusual for buses to be crowded.

Trains An excellent train service, with air-conditioning and announcements in Spanish and English, runs between Málaga and Fuengirola, stopping at the airport, Torremolinos and Arroyo de la Miel. Trains operate every 30 minutes at the airport, in either direction, daily from 06.45 to 23.00. The full journey takes 42 minutes.

HEALTH, SAFETY & CRIME

Pickpockets are common in crowded areas, especially outside monuments and at markets. Be particularly wary of people asking you the time, as they are probably trying to distract you while someone else attempts to snatch your bag or wallet. Use traveller's cheques, Eurocheques or credit cards rather than cash, and carry a photocopy of your passport, leaving the original in the hotel safe. If you have a car, do not leave valuables in view, and try to leave it in a security-controlled car park. In the event of being robbed or attacked, report the incident to the police (*poner una denuncia*) as soon as possible (at least within 24 hours). This is extremely important if you wish to obtain a statement (*denuncia*) to make an insurance claim.

The abundance of street-life means that you will rarely find yourself alone or in a position to be harassed. However, women may be intimidated by men passing comment as they walk by, or even following them. This pastime, known as *piropo*, is common and not meant as a serious threat. Do not use maps late at night, and try to look like you know where you are going. Make sure that you take official taxis displaying a licence number, and avoid public transport at night if alone. Any cab driver touting for business is likely to be illegal.

When in the countryside, you may see signs showing a bull or saying *Toro bravo* (fighting bull). Take these signs seriously – bulls are extremely dangerous and should certainly not be approached.

The biggest danger you are likely to face is overexposure to the sun, particularly from May to October, when temperatures can reach up to 45°C (113°F). Try to avoid walking in the midday sun, and stay in the shade whenever possible. Drink plenty of bottled mineral water. It is advisable to wear sunglasses and a hat when you are out sightseeing.

It is a good idea to stick to bottled water at all times, especially in the summer when the river beds dry up and cause pollutants in the water system to become concentrated. Food in Gibraltar and Spain is as reliable as anywhere else in Europe. Be sensible when eating in Morocco and eat at restaurants that have a high turnover of customers and look clean.

OPENING HOURS

Shops Spanish shops tend to close during the afternoon siesta and on Sundays (except for department stores, shopping malls and touristy souvenir shops in the large towns). Most shops open at 09.30 and close at 13.30. They usually reopen about 17.00 or 17.30 and stay open until 20.30 or 21.00. These times will obviously vary from shop to shop. In Gibraltar, hours are as in the UK, from 09.00 to 17.30. Many close on Sundays.

Museums Hours kept by monuments and museums vary considerably, so it is best to check before you visit. Most close on Sunday afternoons. However, during the tourist season many museums stay open all day.

Churches Most churches open only for Mass, but in small towns a caretaker will often let visitors in between religious services. Mass is held every hour on Sundays, and at about 19.00–21.00 on weekdays. In most churches, tourists are welcome in the church during a service as long as they are quiet. Dress codes are not as strict as in other Catholic countries, but avoid skimpy shorts and bare arms. There is usually no admission charge, although a donation may be expected. In Morocco, entrance to mosques is usually restricted to practising Muslims. If you do enter, keep your shoulders covered and wear a skirt or trousers that come below the knee. Women might also consider covering their heads. **Banks** in Gibraltar are open for business 09.00–15.30 Mon–Thur and 09.00–17.00 Fri. They are closed at the weekend. In Andalucía, banks are open 08.30–14.00 Mon–Fri, and 08.30–13.00 Sat during the winter. From May to September they do not open on Saturdays. Banks are never open on public holidays, and during a town's annual *feria* week the banks will open for just three hours (09.00–12.00), to allow staff to join in the merrymaking.

RELIGION

Gibraltar is largely Catholic with significant Jewish and Muslim populations. Spain is predominantly Catholic and Morocco is Muslim.

TIME DIFFERENCES

Gibraltar and Spain are one hour ahead of Greenwich Mean Time (GMT) and British Summer Time. Morocco is on GMT.

In Spain, the 24-hour clock is used in listings and for official purposes, but not in speech.

TIPPING

Tipping tends to be an issue of discretion in Gibraltar and Spain. A service charge (*servicio*) is usually included in bills, but it is common to tip up to 10 per cent in addition and to give small change to petrol pump attendants, taxi drivers, porters and parking attendants.

TOILETS

Public toilets are scarce, but bars and restaurants in Gibraltar are usually happy to allow you to use theirs, and those in Spain are legally bound to do so. A 'D' on the door stands for *Damas* (ladies), and a 'C' indicates *Caballeros* (men). Keep small change handy because if the toilets are not coin-operated, it is usual to leave some small change for the attendant. In Morocco, toilets are often the squat variety and vary in standards of cleanliness, so use your judgement – although most smart hotels have Western-style facilities. Always carry some toilet paper with you, as it is rarely supplied.

TRAVELLERS WITH DISABILITIES

Modern buildings generally have adequate provision for the disabled, with lifts, ramps and special toilet facilities. However, owing to their construction, entry to certain historical monuments may be restricted. Local tourist offices, or the monument staff, can provide information about wheelchair access.

FIND THE LATEST HOTSPOT

Get more from your holiday and find out the best restaurants, bars, beaches and family-friendly attractions from our handy pocket guides. Our wide range covers up to 45 destinations:

Algarve
Bali
Bulgaria
Corfu
Corsica
Costa Blanca
Costa Brava & Costa Dorada
Costa del Sol & Costa de Almeria
Côte D'Azur
Crete
Croatia
Cuba
Cyprus
Dominican Republic
Egypt
Fuerteventura
Gibraltar
Goa
Gran Canaria
Guernsey
Ibiza
Ionian Islands
Jamaica

Jersey
Lanzarote
Madeira
Mallorca
Malta
Menorca
Mexico
Morocco
Neapolitan Riviera
Orlando
Rhodes & Kos
Santorini
Sardinia
Sicily
Sri Lanka
Tenerife
Thailand
Tunisia
Turkey –
    Aegean Coast
    Lycian Coast
    Mediterranean Coast

Thomas Cook Publishing

ACKNOWLEDGEMENTS

We would like to thank all the photographers, picture libraries and organisations for the loan of the photographs reproduced in this book, to whom copyright in the photograph belongs:
briandaly/BigStockPhoto (page 5), firemansteve/BigStockPhoto (page 99), freeflyer/BigStockPhoto (pages 9, 23); Pictures Colour Library (pages 1, 10–11, 18, 24, 27, 35, 39, 46, 49, 89, 103); Katherine Rushton (pages 32, 65, 67, 87); Photoshot/NHPA (page 13); Photoshot/World Pictures (pages 20, 29, 61, 63, 70, 81, 91, 92); Thomas Cook Tour Operations Ltd (page 51, 56, 79, 104); photononstop/TIPS Images (page 105); Hedwig Storch/Wikimedia Commons (page 96).

Project editor: Catherine Burch
Layout: Julie Crane
Proofreader: Jan McCann
Indexer: Marie Lorimer

Send your thoughts to
books@thomascook.com

- Found a beach bar, peaceful stretch of sand or must-see sight that we don't feature?

- Like to tip us off about any information that needs a little updating?

- Want to tell us what you love about this handy little guidebook and more importantly how we can make it even handier?

Then here's your chance to tell all! Send us ideas, discoveries and recommendations today and then look out for your valuable input in the next edition of this title.

Email to the above address or write to:
HotSpots Series Editor, Thomas Cook Publishing, PO Box 227, Coningsby Road, Peterborough PE3 8SB, UK.